Library of
Davidson College

Edward P. Dozier

Edward P. Dozier
The Paradox of the American Indian Anthropologist

Marilyn Norcini

With a Foreword by Peter M. Whiteley

The University of Arizona Press
Tucson

The University of Arizona Press
© 2007 The Arizona Board of Regents
All rights reserved

Library of Congress Cataloging-in-Publication Data
Norcini, Marilyn, 1950–
Edward P. Dozier : the paradox of the American Indian anthropologist / Marilyn Norcini ; with a foreword by Peter M. Whiteley.
p. cm.
Includes bibliographical references and index.
ISBN-13: 978-0-8165-1790-9 (hardcover : alk. paper)
ISBN-10: 0-8165-1790-8 (hardcover : alk. paper)
1. Dozier, Edward P. 2. Indian anthropologists—Southwest, New—Biography. 3. Indian college teachers—Southwest, New—Biography. 4. Pueblo Indians—Biography. 5. Pueblo Indians—Social life and customs. 6. Kalinga (Philippine people)—Social life and customs. I. Title.
GN21.D69N67 2007
301.092—dc22
[B]
2006025054

Publication of this book is made possible in part by the proceeds of a permanent endowment created with the assistance of a Challenge Grant from the National Endowment for the Humanities, a federal agency.

Manufactured in the United States of America on acid-free, archival-quality paper containing a minimum of 50% post-consumer waste and processed chlorine free.

12 11 10 09 08 07   6 5 4 3 2 1

To my family:
my father, Guy,
my sisters, Missy and Marcia,
and especially my mother,
Dorothy E. Barada Norcini (1920–2001),
as promised

Contents

List of Figures ix

Foreword, by Peter M. Whiteley xi

Preface xv

Prologue: Wake and Funeral of Dr. Edward P. Dozier, 1971 xix

1 The Historical Paradox of the American Indian Anthropologist 3

2 A Multicultural Childhood 15

3 A Linguistic Path to Anthropology 31

4 Fieldwork with Clan Relatives, the Arizona Tewas 55

5 "An Indian and a Scholar" in the Academy 77

6 Fieldwork with the Anthropological Other, the Kalingas 95

7 Leadership in American Indian Studies 113

8 From Paradox to Paradigm 135

Epilogue: Eulogy to Edward P. Dozier, by David Warren 147

Appendixes

A Chronology of the Life of Edward P. Dozier 151

B Edward P. Dozier: A Bibliography 155

C Edward P. Dozier Papers at the Arizona State Museum   161

D Prenuptial Agreement between Thomas S. Dozier and Maria Leocadia Gutierrez, September 25, 1896   163

References   167

Index   177

Figures

1 Thomas and Leocadia Gutierrez Dozier, about 1910   18

2 Leocadia Gutierrez Dozier and her children, 1931   28

3 Edward Dozier in the Army Air Corps, 1941   45

4 Edward Dozier with his daughter Wanda, 1949   58

5 Map showing relationship between Tewa Village in Arizona and Santa Clara Pueblo in New Mexico   60

6 Sheep camp where Dozier lived during Arizona Tewa fieldwork, 1949   64

7 *Newsweek* portrait of Edward Dozier, 1952   78

8 Marianne and Edward Dozier with their children in the Philippines, 1960   100

9 Edward Dozier among Kalinga peacekeepers, 1960   104

10 Edward Dozier on a bridge near a Kalinga village, 1959–60   108

11 Edward P. Dozier, professor of anthropology, 1967   122

Foreword

PETER M. WHITELEY

Anthropology is predicated upon communication across cultural boundaries. The discipline's greatest insights have always come from those most sensitively open to difference, most conscious of its entailments, and those best situated socially and intellectually to discern its key contours. In its modern form, anthropology developed out of the colonial encounter, especially the discovery of the New World, which so utterly startled European thought. Contemplation of a whole new landmass and its myriad peoples, with their ostensibly radical differences from the known world, ushered in the Enlightenment project and the revolution of modernity simultaneously with a bloody legacy of conquest, colonization, and hegemony. The new stories that peoples on both sides of the encounter had to develop to make some sense out of these new Others emerged from exchanges of war, trade, alliance, sometimes mutual engagement, and sometimes bitter estrangement. From the Sepúlveda–Las Casas debate of the sixteenth century to the writings of William Apess and Black Hawk's autobiography in the early nineteenth, to the Handsome Lake religion and the millenarian Ghost Dance, and even to the novels of Leslie Marmon Silko and Sherman Alexie, efforts to explain, dominate, manage, accommodate, and/or purge the Other have echoed through everyday experience, metaphysical thought, and violent conflict over territory in the expanding dominions of new empires and nation-states in the New World.

It is within this framework, broadly speaking, that the anthropological project came to light. Ever since it was formalized in the late nineteenth century, it has been a hybrid inquiry, necessarily pushing the boundaries of received wisdom in its efforts to translate numerous cultural realities. From the first formal monograph, Lewis Henry Morgan's *League of the Ho-dé-no-sau-nee, or Iroquois*, that hybridity of conception and practice has been evident. Morgan's collaborative effort with Ely Parker, Tonawanda Seneca (who went on to become Ulysses S. Grant's aide-de-camp in the Civil War and the first Native American Commissioner of Indian Affairs), was foregrounded in Morgan's dedication of the work to him, calling it "the fruit of our joint researches." Further, several prominent Seneca leaders' own interest in sharing with Morgan the principles of Iroquois political culture played no small part in the project. The contributions of brilliant American Indian successors to Ely Parker—like Francis La Flesche, J.N.B. Hewitt, Arthur C. Parker, and William Jones—have often gone underappreciated in histories of the discipline. But their very interstitiality, passing back and forth across the boundaries of cultural difference, honed their distinctive insights and was responsible for a large part of their respective successes as interpreters of culture. Prominent co-collaborators with non-Native ethnographers, like George Hunt with Franz Boas, were also often determinedly seeking to develop an archive, a consultable record, of their own and neighboring cultures that they feared would otherwise vanish without a trace. The importance of the records they developed is even now insufficiently estimated in the canons of cultural studies. Similarly, later Native ethnographers—like D'Arcy McNickle, Bea Medicine, and Alfonso Ortiz—have been strongly motivated by a desire to preserve the knowledge of traditional cultures both for posterity (their own and the world's) and to defend indigenous social, cultural, and political interests. The passion that such scholars bring to the project transcends disengaged scientific interest with a deep, though often understated, sense of social commitment.

Edward Dozier is a primary exemplar of these patterns, and as Marilyn Norcini cogently demonstrates, was the first professional Native American ethnographer to pursue his calling in a university setting. As the child of an Anglo-American father and a Tewa mother from Santa Clara Pueblo, Dozier was both within and outside traditional circles of knowledge at the Pueblo. But he was reared very much as a member, and he understood the Pueblo Indian world as both a long-term insider and an objective scholar committed to anthropological research. The Pueblos remain very private places, often skeptical of any representations of their society and culture. Dozier's skill in intellectually and socially negotiating and balancing the often opposed worlds of the academy and the community is second to none. His studies of acculturation—and his application of "compartmentalization" to explain the extraordinary ability of Pueblo cultures to persist while partly accommodating to, but without surrendering to, the dominant society's tremendous pressure to change—are a lasting theoretical contribution. Dozier's marvelous ethnography of the Tewa-speaking Pueblo of Hano among the First Mesa Hopi of Arizona lastingly demonstrates the benefits of his "insider/outsider" status superbly. Dozier retained a customary Pueblo modesty and sense of privacy, and it is very fitting that Norcini's intellectual biography does not seek to intrude too far into his personal history while clarifying much of this exemplary Pueblo ethnographer's gifts to the discipline and to the historical and sociocultural record of Pueblo peoples, especially. As a Native pioneer in the sometimes equally closed circles of the academy, Dozier's life and work speak both of and to the importance of anthropology as the most rigorous intellectual medium for explaining peoples and cultures to each other, for an understanding of the human condition in its full variety.

Preface

During a conversation a long time ago, the Cherokee anthropologist Robert K. Thomas asked me, "Why do you want to spend all these years studying someone you've never met and never can meet?" To a historian drawn to biography, the answer is self-evident—it's what historians do. To an anthropologist who is also a historian, it's what I do—my research combines both ethnographic and documentary sources.

As a historian who had returned to graduate school in anthropology at the University of Arizona, I spent a year organizing the Edward P. Dozier papers in the Arizona State Museum archives and studying his formative years (Norcini 1988). This book, therefore, has its documentary roots in an anthropological archive, its academic roots in anthropology, and its ethnographic roots in Santa Clara Pueblo in northern New Mexico, where Edward P. Dozier was born.

After going to Santa Clara Pueblo to meet Dozier's family in the late 1980s, I decided to expand my study to his career as an American Indian anthropologist. Thanks to the Santa Clara Tribal Council and the Dozier family, I spent a year at the pueblo. I conducted additional archival research in family and federal records, along with literature reviews and fifty interviews with native scholars and with Dozier's family, friends, and colleagues. Most Pueblo consultants did not wish to be identified by name, and so I cite them under the general description "Dozier family interview" or "Pueblo interview."

During the 1990s, while doing contract work on applied ethnographic projects for the National Park Service and the Department of Energy, I had the opportunity to work with tribal elders and cultural preservation staff of several Southwestern tribes. I listened and learned about indigenous perspectives toward the anthropologists who had studied their communities during the classic era of American ethnology in the early twentieth century. They critiqued anthropological ethics, research methods, and interpretations and explained the adverse effects of published information on their communities in the past and in the present. Consequently, it was from diverse indigenous consultations that the cultural context of a native anthropologist began to become apparent to me.

When I began researching the professional career of Edward Dozier, my interest was in a history of Native American discourse in anthropology (Norcini 1995). Later, thanks to a summer residency at the School of American Research in 2001 as a William Y. and Nettie K. Adams fellow in the history of anthropology, I changed my focus to the central issue of kinship in the complex identities of indigenous scholars. As a consequence, this book is a critical study of the conflicting contexts that surrounded American Indian anthropologists at mid-twentieth century. Specifically, it is about the structure and meaning of Edward Dozier's relationships with both indigenous and academic communities.

I am well aware of today's growing literature about indigenous issues and by indigenous scholars (e.g., Champagne and Stauss 2002; Champagne, Torjesen, and Steiner 2005; Riley 2004; Smith and Wobst 2005; Wilson and Yellow Bird 2005). Indeed, in my previous research (Norcini 1995) I used writings by several indigenous anthropologists extensively. In this book, however, I focus on the cultural and historical contexts that were relevant to Edward Dozier and make limited use of the broader literature. I recommend the works just cited, among others, to readers who are interested in indigenous studies.

In thanking the many people who assisted me in preparing this book, my gratitude goes first to the Dozier family, who were gracious and patient regarding my research on Edward Dozier—husband, father, and brother. I dedicated my dissertation to them, and with this book I again thank them for their many years of kindness.

I also wish to thank my academic advisors at the University of Arizona, particularly the late Vine Deloria Jr., my teacher, mentor, and friend, along with Robert K. Thomas, Thomas Holm, and Larry Evers in American Indian Studies, my doctoral minor. In the anthropology department at Arizona, I am grateful for the guidance of Ellen B. Basso, Richard Henderson, and the late James E. Officer. I also extend thanks to Christine Szuter and Allyson Carter at the University of Arizona Press for supporting the publication of this book.

In Santa Fe, I wish to remember a close friend and Southwestern anthropologist, the late Charles H. Lange, who introduced me to Pueblo Indian ethnology. He and his wife, Patricia Fogelman Lange, became my extended family in New Mexico. I also thank William Y. and Nettie K. Adams for establishing a fellowship at the School of American Research in the history of anthropology and for recognizing that Edward Dozier holds a unique, previously unrecognized position in the discipline. I acknowledge the constant friendship and collegiality of Richard I. Ford, of the University of Michigan. I thank my talented and good-humored editor, Jane Kepp, for making the editing of the book a valuable learning experience.

I also thank the staff who assisted me in my research at several institutions: Raymond H. Thompson, R. Gwinn Vivian, Alan Ferg, Jeannette Garcia, Susan Luebbermann, Kathleen Hubenschmidt, and Jean Armstrong at the Arizona State Museum, University of Arizona; Garth Bawden, Bruce Huckell, Mari Lyn Salvador, Catherine Baudoin, and Marian Rodee at the Maxwell Museum of Anthropology, University of New Mexico; Scott Rushforth and John Womack at New Mexico State University, Las Cruces; and Richard M. Leventhal, Jeremy A. Sabloff, Robert J. Sharer, and Philip G. Chase at the University of Pennsylvania Museum of Archaeology and Anthropology. My thanks to Peter M. Whiteley, of the American Museum of Natural History, for writing the foreword to this book.

Two important points remain to be mentioned. First, all royalties from the sale of this book are being donated to the Dozier family to establish an educational fund for their children and grandchildren. I hope the book will be part of Edward Dozier's legacy to them. Second, no one in the Dozier family is responsible for the interpretations in this book; that responsibility is mine alone.

Prologue

Wake and Funeral of Dr. Edward P. Dozier, May 5–6, 1971, Española and Santa Clara Pueblo, New Mexico

Bernard Fontana to William Sturtevant, May 10, 1971, National Anthropological Archives, no. 4972 Tewa, Smithsonian Institution

[We—Bernard Fontana, Richard Ford, Keith Basso] arrived at Block's Mortuary about 7:45 [p.m.]. The rosary was being said in English in the chapel of the funeral home. The chapel was about half-filled with people, and Ed's body lay in a gray coffin at the front of the room. The coffin was open from the waist up; the lower portion was draped with an American flag. . . .

By the time Gene [Hodge] and I arrived the rosary was more than half over. . . . It was finished very quickly, and in turn each person got up from his seat and filed past the open coffin. Some looked at Ed and a few knelt by his side for a moment. He had a wooden-beaded rosary clasped in his hands. . . .

We walked quickly by and shook hands with Miguel, Anya, Wanda [Dozier's children], and Marianne [his wife], all of whom had been sitting in a small room off to the side. We met Tom, [one of] Ed's [surviving siblings, four brothers and a sister]; signed the register; and started to leave. Most people, in fact, had already gone when Ed's brother stopped us to say that we were invited to return because the Penitentes from Española had arrived to say another rosary. We went back into the chapel and variously knelt and sat through a rosary in Spanish, spoken with sung responses. . . . The Penitentes were five stately old men, one so old that he could scarcely kneel. Their voices were firm and the words were clear. This time everyone was in the sanctuary of the chapel, including Marianne. The rosario lasted for about 45 minutes, and shortly before it was over, the members of Ed's family were escorted by Tom Dozier—who was clearly in charge of local arrangements—and taken to the side room again to greet those who had not been in church earlier. He said he was surprised when the Penitentes came. The family had not known whether to expect them or not. He was also clearly very pleased about this sudden turn of events. And everywhere in the room one heard Spanish, English, and Tewa being spoken....

By 8:30 the next morning we were at the pueblo, standing outside the atrium wall in front of the church.

It was a beautiful day. Dark clouds rolled slowly up from the south, over the Santa Clara Mountains and up the Rio Grande Valley. In the north and east, toward the Sangre de Cristo Range, the sky was turquoise, dotted here and there by a few advance scouts of the army of rain clouds. The church at Santa Clara Pueblo is small; plastered adobe; and very lovely. The cemetery is within the atrium in the front of the east-facing church; an irrigation ditch, running rapidly with clear water, skirts the northern edge of the church and atrium wall. It fairly sang, much in keeping with the birds who were doing the same thing. The willow and poplar trees were green. The cottonwoods were just beginning to acknowledge spring. When we arrived there were a few other cars and people ahead of us. A large group of men, some in hard hats, sat on the atrium wall above Ed's freshly dug grave. They were talking quietly among themselves, and their mood was anything but somber. A station wagon and a pickup truck came by in a few moments, and the hard-hatted ones climbed in and drove away. The others continued to sit on the wall and talk. Life, for them, was going on as it always had.

More cars came and the crowd grew larger. The anthropologists from the University of New Mexico arrived; more Indians arrived; and Spanish-Americans came. There was one very old Tewa man who stood near the head of the grave, Levi pants, plaid workshirt, and his long hair tied into two braids. There was the carefully bearded Jim Spuhler, dressed in shiny shoes and a fine suit.

And there were Bea Medicine, Jim Wilson, Nibs Hill, Gene Hodge, Charles Loloma's wife, John Adair, Jack Campbell, and many faces totally foreign to me.

The hearse and the limousines arrived with the members of Ed's family and with Dave Warren. The bell in the church tower began to toll the death knell; one ring, fade away, pause, and ring again. A group of Tewas from the pueblo had already gathered inside the church yard, standing next to the Franciscan priest. There was a cross above the arcade of the church. The morning sun stamped its shadow on the east wall of the sacristy. A breeze blew....

Ed's body was taken from the hearse and wheeled into the waiting graveyard. A very crowded graveyard. The casket was lowered into the hole; the bell continued to toll. The black clouds from the south and west were getting closer. The priest read a standard graveside service. There was no Mass; never once did the priest mention Ed by name. Now all the mourners were crowded around the grave site.

Then Dave Warren stood at the head of the grave and gave a eulogy in English. Ed's life, he said, had come full circle. And he spoke of Ed's influence among the lives of all of those of us who knew him. He spoke of Ed's writings, and of how he was not, in fact, gone. He spoke of the impact of a man who had begun in this little pueblo, who had gone into the world and preached his own kind of gospel, and who was now back where it had all started.

He also spoke of the things begun by Ed and which were now on the verge of fruition. And he read from one of the codices what the Nahuatl wisemen had said of death some five hundred years ago. It was something about the earth and about roses.

To the north of where we stood, on the other side of the stream flowing through the village, dozens of children played happily in the schoolyard. Their laughter mingled with the sound of the water in the irrigation ditch and with the sound of the birds.

Paul Tafoya, the governor of the pueblo, spoke next. He was near tears as he gave a eulogy in Tewa. And as he spoke there was the low roll of thunder behind us. The clouds were coming closer. The wind blew a little harder, but there was no dust. It was cool and refreshing.

When Tafoya finished, the workers began to shovel dirt in on the grave. Tom Dozier circulated through the slowly dissolving crowd inviting everyone to his home [actually the Dozier family home] for coffee and doughnuts. We met Ed's other two brothers—both of them looking so much like Ed that it was startling. They shared not only his looks but his mannerisms as well. Tom, on the other hand, is tall, and there is little family resemblance. Ed was the youngest brother.

We drove about two "blocks," if pueblos can be said to have blocks, to Tom's house. There was a large crowd, and by now everyone was very happy. Marianne and her two children knew they had done precisely the right thing. Once in a while we are privileged to be involved in something that is right in every way, and certainly Ed's funeral was that.

And it started to rain. Big drops came down. Everyone was happy about that, too.

Edward P. Dozier

1

The Historical Paradox of the American Indian Anthropologist

Perhaps underlying the traditional anthropological paradigm was an unstated assumption: the observer is a total stranger.
—Kerry D. Feldman, "Anthropology under Contract"

On May 2, 1971, when Edward Pasqual Dozier died of a heart attack in Tucson, Arizona, he was a fifty-five-year-old professor of anthropology at the University of Arizona and at the peak of a twenty-year academic career. He had earned a solid reputation for his research and writing about Pueblo Indian languages and cultures. He had worked in the Pueblo Southwest and in the Philippines, traveled internationally, taught and encouraged university students, published articles and books, and served the interests of tribal communities by promoting Indian higher education. The culmination of his anthropological research was his comparative ethnology *The Pueblo Indians of North America*. Published in 1970, it was a synthesis of the historical, linguistic, and cultural diversity of the Tanoan, Keresan, Zuni, and Hopi communities.

But Dozier was something more than an anthropologist. He was also an American Indian. He was born on April 23, 1916, at Santa Clara Pueblo in northern New Mexico. His mother was a Santa Claran and his father was a Euroamerican ("Anglo" in Southwestern parlance) schoolteacher from Missouri. He was raised in the pueblo until the age of twelve and spoke its Tewa language fluently. Throughout his life Dozier identified himself as a Pueblo Indian.

But in his Indian heritage lay a paradox. In Dozier's time, the expression "American Indian anthropologist" was self-contradictory.

According to contemporary expectations and beliefs about what an anthropologist should be, one could not be an American Indian and an anthropologist at the same time. An anthropologist was an "objective outsider" to the culture being studied.

Yet a paradox, though seemingly contrary to common opinion and sentiment, can also be true. American Indians did become anthropologists, and Edward Dozier was among the earliest to do so. He was the first professionally trained American Indian to develop an academic career in anthropology.

To anthropologists in the mid-twentieth century, an American Indian scholar was an anomaly. The professional standard was that an anthropologist had to come from outside the studied community in order to observe native behavior empirically and interpret it objectively. Kinship in a tribal community automatically disqualified one from being an objective social scientist. From an academic perspective, the paradox of American Indians as anthropologists lay in the opposition between the objectivity of the "outsider" (who could produce an "etic" view of the studied culture) and the subjectivity of the "insider" (who had an "emic" view). Edward Dozier transcended this dichotomy by integrating the two values to some degree in his scholarship on Pueblo Indian culture and language. As a result, he created a relatively more inclusive discourse in anthropology, representing the interests of both tribal and academic communities.

The expression "American Indian anthropologist" was not an oxymoron solely in the academic world. From an indigenous perspective, too, it was self-contradictory. Native people generally believed that one could not be a respected member of a tribe and still share one's tribal knowledge with outsiders, as scientists did. And conservative tribes such as the Southwestern Pueblos were particularly resistant.

Members of Pueblo Indian communities consistently used secrecy to preserve the privileged knowledge of elders, which was passed down in a tradition of oral history. They spoke only from the authority of personal experience. In contrast, anthropologists, working in a literary tradition, wrote authoritative books about other people's knowledge. The two groups' values were antithetical. A Pueblo person acquired knowledge at appropriate times during a lifetime of learning. An anthropologist, on the other hand, came to a village for a short time, asked questions about things he or she did not or should not know, took notes and photographs, and went back to the university to write books. A Pueblo person served the general welfare of the community; an anthropologist served scholarly and public audiences. It was not a Pueblo value for a member to become an anthropologist and study his or her own people for a public readership.

Yet Edward Dozier managed to resolve, to a considerable degree, the "indigenous paradox" as well as the academic one. He created a professional career that correlated his Pueblo values with those of anthropology, and he retained the affection and respect of his community. For the 1950s and 1960s Dozier was a rarity—one of only a handful of minority anthropologists in the academy and the only American Indian professor until 1967. In that year a student whom he had mentored, Alfonso Ortiz of San Juan Pueblo, graduated from the University of Chicago (Ortiz 1969), and John J. Bodine of Taos Pueblo graduated from Tulane University (Bodine 1972).

From the late nineteenth century through much of the twentieth, the typical American anthropologist employed in a university, museum, or government agency was a white male scholar who studied "vanishing" Indian cultures in North America. The popular perception that American Indians were destined to assimilate to the dominant white society created an intellectual climate in which collecting precontact (prereservation) indigenous languages and traditional practices became a race against the clock. Soon, people believed, no evidence of aboriginal life would remain. "Salvage anthropologists" recorded the historical experiences of tribal elders in order to preserve the remnants of native cultures. They asked questions through local interpreters, recorded, cross-checked, and analyzed the information as scientific data, and then published their interpretations in anthropological monographs for audiences of other academics. They regarded as public knowledge not only natives' common knowledge about things such as social organization but also their privileged knowledge of ritual traditions. Anthropologists then disseminated this information about non-Western systems of knowledge through academic, museum, and government channels.

In the production of anthropological knowledge—particularly in ethnology, folklore studies, and linguistics—the participation of American Indians was (and is) essential. During the nineteenth and twentieth centuries anthropologists depended heavily on American Indians in their fieldwork, employing or consulting them for data collection, language translation, and explanation of native meanings. Consequently, the historical roles of American Indians and anthropologists were defined early in a young discipline seeking respectability and professional identity in the academy.

The scientific model of objectivity prescribed the roles that American Indians played—those of guides, interpreters, and sources. Those roles ensured that the anthropologist maintained a social and intellectual distance from the natives. This social hierarchy arose from a tradition of colonial relations of power between governing institutions, cultural brokers, and indigenous people. In the custom of scholarly research, the anthropologist was not an Indian. He was an objective scholar from the dominant society, an educated Westerner who possessed intellectual curiosity, a commitment to social science research, and a spirit of adventure for faraway places. Anthropologists were the antithesis of kin; they were strangers investigating alien cultures.

The concept of an American Indian becoming an anthropologist, then, was paradoxical. Indians, the dominant paradigm maintained, do not ask the questions; they answer and translate the questions. Indians do not write about their own kin and cultures; nonmembers write about them. Indians provide oral accounts; they do not write or publish texts. Indians may translate native language texts, but they work under the supervision of anthropologists. With the significant exception of the more collaborative anthropological practices begun by Franz Boas and continued by his students, to which I return later, Indian assistants were generally anonymous. Their names were absent from professional monographs on American Indian culture, language, biology, and archaeology.

For indigenous people, the paradox of the American Indian anthropologist rested in large part on the way cultural knowledge was (and is) transmitted and preserved across generations through oral traditions. Young people learned from their elders and passed knowledge on to their children and grandchildren. Learning about native plants, for example, began during childhood, and it took a lifetime to be able to correctly identify, collect, preserve, and use plants for the benefit of the community. Traditional plant knowledge was not written in a book, nor could it have been understood in one reading. Cultural knowledge was specialized; not everyone knew how to gather, process, and use plants correctly. Doing so involved ritual prayers in the native language. Gaining wisdom took patience, care, presence in the community, and a respectful attitude.

The organization of scientific knowledge in academic anthropology ran contrary to traditional Pueblo Indian ways of knowing. Anthropological methods were incompatible with indigenous models of education. Accordingly, a book offering encyclopedic information about the Pueblos' cultural landscape, such as John P. Harrington's 1916 *Ethnogeography of the Tewa Indians,* was inconsistent with traditional constructions of privileged and specialized knowledge. No one person possessed (or should possess) all the information; it was deliberately diffused throughout the village in the specialized knowledge and expertise of certain individuals. The cultural strategy was (and is) that the death of one person should not threaten the preservation of all cultural knowledge, but only a portion of it.

Many Pueblo Indian people regarded books, unlike speech, as fixed and static. Books threatened traditional systems of knowledge, in part because they revealed oral knowledge without any indigenous understanding of how to use and respect its inherent power. Books made public the specialized oral traditions normally controlled by a few select specialists. Their authors recorded these traditions in literary form and then distributed them to persons outside the native culture.

Anthropologists writing books about Pueblo Indians usually kept silent concerning who had provided them with information. They used pseudonyms and anonymous sources to protect "informants" and their extended families against retribution by other community members. Yet anonymity also raised a barrier for leading elders, who, when they read the books or had them read to them, had no way to assess the informants' accuracy, competence, or right to privileged knowledge. Therefore, anonymity obstructed critical reviews of books by knowledgeable persons in the studied communities.

Because the American Indian as anthropologist was a paradox in both American Indian culture and academic anthropology, native scholars were rare exceptions in the early years of the discipline and indeed are still relatively rare—despite the fact that anthropology in the United States was founded on research conducted in American Indian societies. The double bind for native scholars was the sum of the differences between a Western society based upon the individual and an indigenous society based upon the community. The two groups' systems of knowledge, for example, were constructed upon contrary models of intellectual property—the Western model of knowledge as alienable property belonging to the individual and the American Indian model of knowledge as inalienable property belonging to the community. Western social values include private ownership of property, holding of land in severalty, personal initiative and independence, personal wealth, and the nuclear family. American Indian social values include communal use of property, holding of land in common, community work, interdependence and reciprocity, redistributive wealth, and cultural survival. When these different systems converge on American Indians who are also anthropologists, they experience a double bind of competing cultural responsibilities. They face the challenge of creating scholarship that simultaneously meets Western and American Indian standards.

American Indian anthropologists were (and are) tribal members who worked in museums, government, and universities, generally at a distance from their kin and community. These native scholars frequently became suspect in their own communities—for the objects they collected, the narrative texts they translated, and the traditional knowledge they published. Although a segment of the community might have supported the scholars' careers, the prevalence of factionalism in American Indian communities generally guaranteed native anthropologists a counterforce of criticism. It was not uncommon for some tribal members to imagine that successful people working in off-reservation jobs had compromised their community's values. Consequently, the American Indian in anthropology frequently worked on the margins of both academe and the tribe.

Edward Dozier was not the first American Indian to face the double paradox of native and scholar. In the late nineteenth and early twentieth centuries, a few Western-educated American Indians had been employed in anthropological museums (Hinsley 1981). They included the folklorist J.N.B. Hewitt (Tuscarora) at the Smithsonian Institution's Bureau of American Ethnology (BAE); the ethnologist Francis La Flesche (Omaha), also at the BAE; the ethnologist William Jones at the Field Museum of Natural History; the archaeologist Arthur C. Parker (Seneca) at the American Museum of Natural History, the New York State Museum, and later (as director), the Rochester Museum of Arts and Sciences; and assistant curator Louis Shotridge (Tlingit) at the University of Pennsylvania Museum of Archaeology and Anthropology.

Most American Indian museum employees were assigned to collect artifacts and native language texts in the area of their cultural affiliation. Louis Shotridge, for instance, collected significant Northwest Coast artifacts for the University of Pennsylvania Museum. Like other Indian employees, he occupied an ambiguous position and held an ambivalent identity relative to the institution and his community. Proud of the artistic and cultural achievements of his people, he was committed to collecting and exhibiting sacred materials for the museum (Seaton 2001). But he was also conflicted over ethical issues surrounding his removal of "highly esteemed object[s]" from the community (Shotridge 1929:341). In one of his published articles he described his cultural and professional dilemma upon acquiring for the museum a rare Tlingit shark helmet from the Kaguanton clan: "It is true that the modernized part of me rejoiced over my success in obtaining this important ethnological specimen for the Museum, but, as one who had been trained to be a true Kaguanton, in my heart I cannot help but have the feeling of a traitor who has betrayed confidence" (Shotridge 1929:343).

The federal Office of Indian Affairs (later the Bureau of Indian Affairs, or BIA) also employed educated American Indians as civil servants. They worked on projects comparable to those of today's applied anthropologists, such as tribal government reorganization. Their aim was to be of service to American Indian communities through their government work. Examples of such early federal workers were Lee Marmon (Laguna Pueblo), Henry Roe Cloud (Winnebago), Archie Phinney (Nez Perce, a student of Boas's), and D'Arcy McNickle (Flathead–Salish). With no college education but with an honorary doctorate from the University of Colorado, McNickle moved to Canada, near his home reservation, and established a department of anthropology at the University of Saskatchewan in Regina (Parker 1992). Unlike Dozier, however, McNickle was not an academic anthropologist.

By far the largest numbers of American Indians who were engaged in anthropology in the early years of the discipline were linguistic field assistants (Norcini 1995). Although more than a few native speakers assisted Columbia University professor Franz Boas, he worked most closely with a select number of American Indians—Ella Cara Deloria (Lakota), George Hunt (Kwakiutl), Henry W. Tate (Tsimshian), and Charles Cultee (Kathlamet). These collaborators worked in the American historical tradition by collecting, transcribing, translating, and publishing narratives from elders in tribal communities. Boas's students followed this pattern. Edward Sapir (Darnell 1990) collaborated on American Indian linguistics with Frances Johnson (Takelma), Tony Tillohash

(Southern Ute), Charlie Mack (Unitah Ute), John Whitney (Sarcee), and Alex Thomas (Nootka). Others recorded American Indian life histories—for example, Ruth Underhill with Maria Chona (Papago-Tohono O'odham) and Paul Radin with the Blowsnake family (Winnebago).

What was remarkable about the Boasian anthropologists was that they, with their mentor, began a new academic tradition in which American Indian contributors were acknowledged by name in anthropological publications. This was an innovation in the young discipline. In their monographs on native language texts, these anthropologists identified their American Indian colleagues as field collectors on title pages, in acknowledgments, and in introductions (Norcini 1995). Some Indian fieldworkers became coauthors with Boas (see Boas and Deloria 1941; Boas and Hunt 1905-6). Although they worked outside the academy, a few American Indian scholars eventually became sole authors of texts on their own cultural communities (for example, Deloria 1932; Jones 1907).

Edward Dozier did not follow a career in museum or government work, but he was not unlike his predecessors in that he faced stereotypical roles as an American Indian in anthropology. He was fortunate, however, in living at a time when greater educational opportunities were available to him. The financial support of federal loans, the GI Bill, a new philanthropic foundation for minority scholars, and social science grants helped him bridge the barriers that American Indian students faced in higher education. With these benefits and with the support of his mentors, Dozier, unlike many native scholars before him, was able to enter the academy directly from graduate school, negotiate the dual pressures of traditional culture and social science, and create a successful career in anthropology.

Indeed, Dozier was able to transcend a portion of the academic paradox by making his cultural affiliation an asset in his research. Whereas his kinship with the communities he studied might have disqualified him as a scientist, he managed to use that very kinship to gain a unique entry into those communities, gather information that might have been inaccessible to someone else, and thereby legitimate himself as a scientist. As he wrote in *The Pueblo Indians of North America,* "The information contained in this case study is the result of a lifetime spent among the Pueblos. Although I was born and grew up in the pueblo of Santa Clara and still consider it my home, I have lived in or visited every village small and large, from the Hopi towns of lower and upper Moencopi in Arizona to the double apartment buildings of Taos Pueblo in northern New Mexico" (Dozier 1970a:xi). He was welcomed as a kinsman in all of them.

Dozier's approach to culture—like that of other Boasians of his time and of his fellow anthropologists since—was to record the distinctive practices of each community and to interpret behavior within its historical and cultural contexts. Shared human qualities and the universal value of humanity were frequent themes in his ethnology. Even when studying the divisive aspects of Pueblo factionalism, he emphasized communities' accomplishments in adapting and enduring amid conflict (Dozier 1966c). As early as his research for his dissertation at the University of California–Los Angeles, he interpreted social change at Tewa Village on the Hopi reservation as a functional means for its people to survive with their language and core identity intact. Later in his career, after working in the Philippines, he attempted to demystify the Kalinga people of northern Luzon, who had long been stereotyped as savage headhunters. He interpreted cultural changes as pragmatic and necessary adaptations by enduring communities. He did so in a quiet, unassuming way that proved effective with diverse people.

Thanks in part to Edward Dozier's pioneering experience, the historical paradox of the American Indian anthropologist has been addressed and redefined in the social sciences—especially as a result of efforts by native faculty, beginning in the late 1960s, to build an academic base in interdisciplinary American Indian Studies programs. The indigenous paradox has persisted, but with a gradual change in attitudes toward community-based academic research as new generations of American Indian college graduates have used scholarship in several disciplines to resolve contemporary issues. Looking back, we can begin to appreciate the contributions of Edward P. Dozier. He transcended the dichotomy expressed in the phrase "caught between two worlds" and made substantial strides toward introducing native cultural values into academic life and scholarship.

2

A Multicultural Childhood

Heritage is . . . more than possessions, either tangible or intangible. The most important aspect of a heritage is that it is a design for living; it gives us direction and purpose in life.
—Edward P. Dozier, keynote address,
Fifth Annual Navajo Youth Conference

The people who celebrated Edward Dozier's life and mourned his death at his funeral in 1971 were Pueblo Indians, Spanish Americans, and Anglos, an assortment of family members, friends, and professional colleagues. They reflected the multicultural world in which Dozier had lived and worked. His mother, Leocadia Gutierrez Dozier (ca. 1875–1950), was a Tewa Pueblo Indian from Santa Clara, New Mexico. His father, Thomas Sublette Dozier (1857–1925), was an Anglo from St. Louis, Missouri. The two made an unusual and successful marriage in which each honored the other's cultural beliefs and customs. They raised their eleven children to be equally respectful of others. Their youngest child, Edward, would eventually find this heritage in diverse cultures to be the foundation that mediated the inherent paradox of the American Indian anthropologist.

Thomas S. Dozier came to New Mexico Territory in 1893, in the midst of a career change. Because business at his Midwestern law practice had been slow, he had drawn on his prior experience as a country schoolteacher in Missouri and Illinois, taken a civil service test, and become qualified as a teacher in the Indian Service. At the time, most job vacancies for government schoolteachers lay in the West. In New Mexico Territory during the 1890s, a number of grade schools were established for Pueblo Indian children. Sister Mary Katharine Drexel, from Philadelphia, founded St. Catherine's School, a popular Catholic boarding school in Santa Fe, in 1894. The federal government also established day schools on Indian reservations and started an off-reservation boarding school, the Santa Fe Indian School, in 1890.

Thomas Dozier was assigned to the Pueblo Indian day schools. From 1893 through 1898 he served as one of the earliest teachers at the Santa Clara Pueblo day school, and later he opened the first day school at San Ildefonso Pueblo (NARA, RG 75, Civil Archives Division, Thomas S. Dozier file, NAB). He taught grade-school students at Santa Clara in a government-leased room at Pedro Baca's family house, and at San Ildefonso Pueblo, in the governor's house, which was remodeled by Indian carpenters at federal expense (EPD1.4, 1914).

When Thomas Dozier arrived at Santa Clara in 1893 he was thirty-five years old and single. He entered a Tewa community of 225 persons (U.S. Census of 1890, Department of Interior, 1894) that organized its residents according to a principle of duality—a moiety system. Under this system two groups, the Summer and Winter sides, alternately managed the village's ceremonial and civil life within a seasonal ritual cycle. The Summer side governed from the spring to the fall equinox, and the Winter side, from the fall to the spring equinox. Each member of the pueblo belonged to one of the moieties, generally (but not exclusively) through descent on the father's side (Ortiz 1965).

To incorporate Thomas Dozier into the kinship structure of the village, the Agapito Naranjo family, of the Winter side, adopted him as its son. He was given the Tewa name Thang Pii, meaning "sun rise," a term appropriate for someone who came from the east. He lived with the Naranjos under their firm instruction never to write about Pueblo religious life, although he did write general stories about his early experiences living in the pueblos during the 1890s. His hometown newspaper in Missouri, the *Cameron Sun,* published his writings in a three-part series in 1894 (EPD1.5, 1894; T.S. Dozier 1894). Later in life he wrote articles on a variety of Southwestern topics, some of which were published in newspapers or magazines (e.g., T.S. Dozier 1921) but many of which were never published.

Thomas Dozier's future wife, Leocadia, was the daughter of José Domingo Gutierrez and María Antonia (Tonita) Silva, also of the Winter side and members of the Badger clan. Raised a devout Catholic, she was known by her Spanish name, Maria Lucaria Gutierrez; her Tewa name was P'oo kwi tsawaa, "the blueness of a lake" (Dozier family communication). In the past, Franciscan missionaries had given Catholic baptismal names to Pueblo converts, along with Spanish middle names and surnames, in order to assimilate native practices to European forms. Over time, certain Spanish surnames became associated with specific pueblos. At Santa Clara, common family names included Gutierrez, Naranjo, and Tafoya. In turn, the Pueblo people modified the pronunciation of Spanish names to correspond to local language sounds, creating uniquely different names (Dozier 1956a).

In the late nineteenth century, prior to Thomas Dozier's arrival, factionalism had divided Santa Clara Pueblo into three competitive parties—the Summer side, the main Winter side, and a progressive Winter side. Leocadia Gutierrez's family belonged to the main Winter side, but her half-brother, Vidal Gutierrez, was the head of the progressive Winter group. This splinter group believed in general elections for tribal officers, freedom to choose whether or not to participate in ritual dances, and the right to farm one's land as one thought best (for example, when to plant and harvest crops). Historically, members of the progressive faction had rebelled against the conservative faction's enforcement of customary laws (such as compulsory community labor on public works) and rule by caciques, or indigenous "chiefs" (refer to Juan V. Silva and Jesus Silver depositions in Hill 1982:193–94). Because Leocadia's family belonged to the main Winter group, it was the group the Doziers' children followed.

Leocadia Gutierrez was eighteen when Thomas Dozier came to

Figure 1. Thomas Sublette Dozier and Leocadia Gutierrez Dozier with their eighth child, Federico Antonio, born on November 20, 1909. This photograph was taken in 1910 in Guachepangue, a Pueblo-Spanish settlement adjacent to Santa Clara Pueblo, where the Doziers built an adobe house for their growing family. (Photograph courtesy of the Dozier family)

live at Santa Clara. She never attended the government day school; her role, as the family's eldest daughter, was to care for her younger siblings—to take them to and from school but never to be schooled herself. How Thomas and Leocadia met or what drew them to each other is unknown, but apparently they courted and then married according to local tradition. The family record book states that "according to Pueblo custom this marriage was consecrated more than two months before the performance of the rites of the church" (Dozier family record book). Soon afterward, Leocadia decided to have a church wedding (EPD1.1, José Domingo Gutierrez to Cosme Herrera, September 24, 1896). She and Thomas were married "in the Chapel of the Pueblo of Santa Clara, on the 28th of September 1896, by the Reverend Father Francisco Guyos" (Dozier family record book).

The Dozier-Gutierrez union came with a bundle of federal conditions. An 1888 congressional statute (25 U.S. Statutes at Large 392) regulated marriages between Indian women and white men. It had been written to protect the property rights of Indian women who married white U.S. citizens. The law limited the property rights a white man could gain by marrying an Indian woman, whose tribal land was nontaxable. The federal law stated:

> *Be it enacted...* That no white man, not otherwise a member of any tribe of Indians, who may hereafter marry, an Indian woman, member of any Indian tribe in the United States, or any of its Territories except the five civilized tribes in the Indian Territory, shall by such marriage hereafter acquire any right to any tribal property, privilege, or interest whatever to which any member of such tribe is entitled.
>
> Sec. 2. That every Indian woman, member of any such tribe of Indians, who may hereafter be married to any citizen of the United States, is hereby declared to become by such marriage a citizen of the United States, with all the rights, privileges, and immunities of any such citizen, being a married woman: *Provided*, that nothing in this act contained shall impair or in any way affect the right or title of

such married woman to any tribal property or any interest therein. (25 U.S. Statutes at Large 392, quoted in Prucha 1975:176–77)

The U.S. law guaranteed that Leocadia Gutierrez, as a member of Santa Clara Pueblo, would preserve her tribal property rights. Her non-Indian husband had no claim on her tribal assets. Moreover, upon her marriage to Thomas Dozier, Leocadia Gutierrez became a United States citizen—twenty-eight years earlier than most other Santa Clarans, who became citizens through the U.S. Indian Citizenship Act of 1924 (43 U.S. Statutes at Large 253). When the Doziers' children were born, they simultaneously became U.S. citizens and members of Santa Clara Pueblo. Significantly, all the Dozier children acquired their tribal birthright before a controversial 1939 ordinance that changed the pueblo's membership rule from bilateral descent (that is, from either the mother or the father) to patrilineal descent (from the father only).

Most unusually, Thomas and Leocadia signed a prenuptial agreement just before their Catholic wedding. It is a unique legal document in Indian-white history—an early, if not the first, legal record of a marriage between an Anglo and a member of Santa Clara Pueblo. The motivation for this formal document, according to the Dozier family, was that the Catholic Church required an official confirmation when a non-Catholic married a Catholic, to ensure that the non-Catholic spouse would not interfere with the Catholic spouse's practice of her faith or raising of the couple's children as Catholics. The rarity of the document reflects the infrequency of marriages between Catholics and Protestants at Santa Clara Pueblo in the nineteenth century. The Dozier family assumes that Leocadia and Thomas discussed the document, and because it seems to exceed the standard obligations, Thomas Dozier may have added additional rights and obligations to his future wife. Dozier, a trained lawyer, was probably familiar with the 1888 congressional statute.

The complete text of the prenuptial agreement, signed on September 25, 1896, was written in both English and Spanish (see appendix D). In brief, it stipulated that Thomas—in addition to acknowledging Leocadia's property rights under federal law—agreed "to maintain and keep" her as "his lawful wife in every respect as if she were of his own race." He agreed to provide a home for her on the Santa Clara reservation and "not to remove nor influence [her] to remove from the said Reservation . . . against her will." He promised not to interfere in her practice of her religious and cultural beliefs or to attempt to have their children "taught a different religious belief" from hers.

Leocadia, in turn, agreed to be "a faithful wife" and to respect "any rules, customs, rites or ceremonies now pertaining to [Thomas] . . . by reason of his religious belief or previous training." (He had been baptized by a Methodist Episcopal bishop in Missouri.) Any property he might acquire outside the reservation boundaries would "be governed by the laws of descent of the place" where that property was situated. That is, it came under New Mexico territorial jurisdiction. Because the agreement ensured Leocadia the right to raise her children according to Pueblo beliefs, it became a significant factor in shaping the Pueblo Indian identity of Edward Dozier and his siblings.

Years later, Thomas S. Dozier reflected on his marriage and enumerated his many children in a letter to his cousin, Dr. L.C. Toney, in the Midwest:

> I think you know I married a Pueblo Indian woman. She had not even had any advantages of school. Yet with all her disadvantages—her lack of training and different ways from my own, I am still quite proud of her. I married her in the fall of 1896 and she has born me eleven children. We lost our oldest boy of smallpox in his 3rd year and our 10th child of Pneumonia in 1914. My 3 oldest boys, Guadalupe Pitman, Jose Pablo, Luis Tomas, are 20, 18 and 17 years, respectively. Then came my two girls, Carolina—14 and Ramona—13. Then, 4 boys, Miguel (Mitchel), Federico (Frederick), David (David), and Edwardo de Pascual, so named because he was born on Easter Sunday, '16. You will

note that all have been given Spanish names. This for the reason that their mother's people are Roman Catholics and the Church has from very early times been ruled by Spanish-speaking priests similar to the California missions. While my wife and family use invariably at home their own Tegua dialect their worship is in the language of the Mexican people. As far as possible I speak English to the children but among themselves they persist in the use of their old Tegua. Of course, all of them learn Spanish from their daily intercourse with the Mexican people. None of us have any extensive association with other than the Mexican people. (EPD1.1, T.S. Dozier to L.C. Toney, December 1919)

From documents and interviews, it remains unclear whether Thomas S. Dozier could speak the Tewa language. According to family members, he tried to learn it when he was first married. Alice Marriott, in her book *Maria: The Potter of San Ildefonso,* wrote that Dozier "learned Tewa from his wife, and he often used it in speaking to the school children" (Marriott 1948:81). In his newspaper and magazine articles about Pueblo Indians, he frequently used Tewa words to explain the culture and portray an authentic Indian Southwest (Norcini 1995:53–63). Leocadia did not speak English, although a member of the Dozier family suggested that she might have understood it but deliberately chose not to speak it (Dozier family interview, May 9, 1988). In any case, in the Doziers' everyday lives, Spanish became their lingua franca. Documents preserved over the couple's twenty-nine-year marriage (EPD1.1, Lucaria Gutierrez de Dozier to Señor Tomás Dozier, July 19, 1900), together with their bilingual prenuptial agreement, attest to their use of Spanish to communicate.

In 1898 Thomas S. Dozier left government service. He explained to his cousin that his reason for leaving was his "constitutional tendency to nervousness" (EPD1.1, T.S. Dozier to L.C. Toney, December 1919). He also wrote that he was unable to accept another position far away because his wife, "being a native

Santa Clara woman could not consent to a removal from her home pueblo for any great distance" (NARA, RG 75, Civil Archives Division, T.S. Dozier to Dr. Hailman, 4 February 1897, NAB). From this time until his death in 1925 he held a variety of jobs in an effort to support his large family. He collected and sold American Indian and Mexican "curios" until 1913. He also pursued an avocational interest in ethnology by collecting artifacts and related cultural information in the late 1890s for prominent museum anthropologists such as Frederick Webb Hodge, of the Bureau of American Ethnology, and Stewart Culin, of the Free Museum of Science and Art (later the University Museum at the University of Pennsylvania) (EPD1.1, Hodge to T.S. Dozier, February 17, 1896; Culin to T.S. Dozier, December 28, 1898). For this fieldwork he was repaid in BAE books by Hodge and with a citation in Culin's publication (Culin 1907:368–69). In his later years, from 1915 through 1917, Thomas Dozier farmed and unsuccessfully tried to earn a living by writing on Southwestern topics. He died of a heart attack in 1924 at the Thompson Ranch in Fairview, New Mexico, and was buried at Santa Clara Pueblo.

Edward was the Doziers' eleventh and last child. He was delivered in Leocadia's parents' house in Santa Clara on Easter Sunday, April 23, 1916. Two months later, in accordance with the prenuptial agreement, he was baptized a Roman Catholic. A priest named Father Halterman christened him with the Spanish name Eduardo de Pasqual (Easter) Dozier. His godfather was José Domingo Naranjo, the son of Agapito Naranjo, with whom Thomas Dozier had lived when he first arrived at the pueblo. Like his brothers, sisters, and other Santa Clara children, Edward also received an Indian name from his mother's relatives a few days after he was born. His name in the Tewa language was Awa see Tsire, meaning "cattail jay bird" or "marsh bird" (Dozier family communication, 2005).

Edward spent most of his childhood years in the pueblo. Although from 1923 to 1926 he attended the first through third grades at a nearby Santa Fe County public school, his experience with non-Indians other than his father and his business friends was limited. And Edward was shy. In a rare autobiographical comment, he wrote about his Pueblo boyhood experiences during the 1920s and 1930s:

> Interaction with neighboring non-Indian population was minimal until the age of twelve and rather painful since we could communicate only with extreme difficulty in English language. Knowledge of the White world was so poor that we as a family felt inadequate to cope with it and withdrew (as Pueblo Indians, generally) into the familiar and secure patterns of our Pueblo culture. My father passed away when I was nine: the very year that I began school in the Pueblo Day School. (EPD 4.5, Dozier to Marian Gridley, January 30, 1959)

After his father's death, Edward attended fourth and fifth grades at the Santa Clara day school, from the fall of 1926 to the summer of 1928. In the school censuses for December 1926 and June 1927 he was listed as the only non-full-blood student among approximately fifty children. The following December he was one of five, and in June 1928, one of four (NARA, RG 75, NPA, General Correspondence, School Census Reports, 1904–37, RM).

The school census and curriculum reflected the government's Indian "civilization regulations" of the 1880s to early 1930s. These federal administrative policies outlawed Indian language, dress, arts, and religion, including Pueblo Indian dances. Dozier experienced the later years of this systematic policy of assimilating Indians into the dominant, English-speaking society. Speaking one's native language was not permitted in a government day school, as Dozier remembered:

> The schools were conducted in English. . . . it was a combination of vocational work and classroom instruction taught unsatisfactorily by teachers who coerced us into our studies and tried to stamp out everything that was Indian. As a result we learned English poorly and digested very little of the subject matter. Every time discipline was re-

laxed we lapsed into our familiar native idiom and of course persisted to communicate in Tewa in the playground and outside of school. I learned English and began to appreciate schools only after being sent off to a Catholic School in Santa Fe. . . . In my school surroundings after the age of twelve, there were no Tewa speakers, hence I was forced to learn English rapidly and became quickly immersed in the dominant White culture. (EPD4.1, Dozier to Gridley, January 30, 1959)

As a Pueblo child, Edward learned from the role models he saw all around him a set of cultural values about what being a "good" Tewa person entailed. For one thing, it meant following a norm of reciprocity. In all one's actions, "for each thing taken, something should be returned" (Naranjo 1992:98). Before a potter took clay from the earth, for example, she said a prayer of thanks to Clay Mother (Naranjo-Morse 1992). It also meant following an ethos of "seeking life" (Laski 1958). That is, a good Tewa was to live a life filled with inspiration, fueled by labor and a thoughtful approach (Naranjo-Morse 1992:15). One was to seek beauty and harmony with one's human and spiritual communities, gaining knowledge, wisdom, and wholeness through traditional ways of learning (Cajete 1994:34).

As the anthropologist Vera Laski described it, the supreme aspiration of a Tewa person was "to be loved by the gods [and] to be liked by one's fellow men" (Laski 1958:89). She explained the spirit of being Tewa: "While the Great Ones may bestow, upon those who are worthy, the blessings of being loved by the gods, one must also deserve and acquire, through proper conduct of living, the status of being liked by one's fellow men. Thus, the ultimate wish and prayer becomes also the supreme law of personal conduct" (Laski 1958:89–90).

From interviews with Pueblo people, archival documents, and anthropological accounts both by Indians and by non-Indians such as Laski, a useful, albeit essentialized, profile of the "ideal" Rio Grande Tewa can be drawn. In general, a Tewa person was polite and respectful to elders; hardworking and generous; observant of reciprocal relations in social and spiritual interactions; respectful of natural cycles of life and death for all forms of life (including people, animals, plants, houses, rocks, and other objects); conservative and modest; cooperative with others, seldom acting independently; protective of traditional cultural knowledge; a speaker of the Tewa language; and, consequently, someone loved or liked by all.

Dozier himself, years later, described the Tewa personality as unaggressive and inconspicuous (Dozier 1958c). A Pueblo Indian could be stoic and impassive, he wrote, masking "the turmoil within," which "made him difficult to analyze by the white man" (EPD3.1, Dozier to Sergeant, September 5, 1934). According to Dozier, a key feature of the Pueblo personality was a "reluctance to be assertive and conspicuous," which produced a way of speaking characterized by a "subdued oratorical style" (Dozier 1958c: 272).

Very likely these characterizations were self-reflexive comments describing Dozier's own self-effacing and modest demeanor. As a child he seems to have absorbed the values of his community and developed a personality compatible with Tewa values. Indeed, in later years his friends and colleagues confirmed that his observations applied equally to himself. A Pueblo person remembered Edward Dozier as a kind and pleasant man (Pueblo interview, December 10, 1990). A colleague at the University of Arizona remembered

> a shy, kind of retiring side to the man, which hid a great deal. He didn't talk very much. He certainly never talked to fill up empty interactional space. He rarely asked pointed questions. It was hard to hold his eyes with yours in a gaze that lasted more than two or three seconds. . . . He hardly ever raised his voice. He was an expert listener. And at faculty meetings, for example, [he] would typically wait until everyone had their say on an issue before chiming in with an opinion or opinions of his own.
>
> And I think that if I thought about it, I could develop

even further the notion that his inner personal manner was in many ways deeply Indian. He simply didn't accomplish the business of social interaction like a lot of his colleagues did. And this more than anything else I think led to the impression that he was shy and retiring. (Keith Basso, interview, May 12, 1993)

Emil Haury, the chairman of the Department of Anthropology at Arizona who hired Dozier there, remembered his cultural reserve: "Although he had made a wonderful adjustment from . . . Pueblo life to our culture (he was well educated and well versed in anthropology), there was a certain reticence about him that I would associate with his Indian past" (Emil Haury, interview, June 5, 1990).

Being a "good Tewa" would not necessarily make life in the Anglo and Hispanic Southwest easier for Edward, and at the age of twelve he entered that world for the remainder of his youth. By the time he was ready to begin sixth grade, his mother had moved the family to Albuquerque, where he attended public school for a year. His older brothers and his older sister Caroline worked for wages outside the reservation to support their mother and younger siblings. They paid the cost of tuition so that Edward could attend St. Michael's College, a private Catholic high school operated by the Christian Brothers in Santa Fe. His mother and some of the other children moved to Santa Fe during that time, so that he could commute daily to school.

Edward Dozier was a Pueblo Indian boy at a predominantly Hispanic school. His classmates singled him out as an Indian by calling him "Chief." Dozier wrote long afterward: "School experiences for Pueblo Indians of my generation and earlier ones were essentially unpleasant whether in the Day or Boarding schools. . . It is not surprising therefore, that there was little encouragement to acquire an education; motivations came from the individual involved and not from relatives and the Indian community" (EPD 4.5, Dozier to Gridley, January 30, 1959). During his seven years at the off-reservation school, Dozier received a liberal arts education. He did well academically in languages (Latin, French, Spanish),

Figure 2. Portrait of the Dozier family taken at Mack Studio in Santa Fe, New Mexico, 1931. Seated: Tom, Leocadia, David. Standing: Edward, Mike, Ramona, Caroline, Paul, Pete. The family moved to Santa Fe in 1929 so that Edward could attend St. Michael's College, a high school operated by the Christian Brothers. (Photograph courtesy of the Dozier family)

received an achievement medal in English (EPD2.4, Dozier to Bronson, January 1, 1935), and served as assistant editor of the school paper during his senior year.

Dozier graduated from St. Michael's in 1935. Toward the end of his high school experience he began to benefit from federal financial support for higher education, implemented as part of the Indian New Deal by John Collier, commissioner of Indian affairs under Franklin D. Roosevelt. Educational reform policies were part of the 1934 Wheeler-Howard Act, commonly known as the Indian Reorganization Act, or IRA (48 U.S. Statutes at Large 984). With it Congress attempted to correct some of the erosion of tribal self-governance and traditional cultural values that had resulted from earlier legislation. A hallmark of the Indian Reorganization Act was the end of the federal government's "allotment" policy, by which Indian reservations were broken up into plots and assigned to individuals under private, rather than collective, ownership. This earlier allotment legislation did not apply to the Pueblos, because they owned their land in fee simple title (Cohen 1941).

Other sections of the IRA addressed the promotion of cross-cultural education, the writing of tribal constitutions and charters for economic development, and the provision of reimbursable loans that could be used for higher education. Dozier credited the Collier administration's Indian reforms: "Changes in policies and attitudes ushered in by the Collier regime modified the situation dramatically. I benefited from this change toward the end of my secondary school education and of course the younger generations of Pueblo Indians have generally not experienced the unpleasant aspects of Indian schools" (EPD 4.5, Dozier to Gridley, January 30, 1959).

Although the large Dozier family had moved frequently for economic reasons—even before Thomas Dozier's death—it maintained an unbroken relationship over the years with Santa Clara Pueblo and with Leocadia's relatives there. Despite attending public and private schools away from the pueblo, Edward remained firmly connected to his Santa Clara community through kinship and language. Nevertheless, it remains uncertain whether or not he participated in Pueblo ceremonial life as a child. One's ceremonial status is not a topic Pueblo people commonly discuss with outsiders. When consultants do make statements about someone's ceremonial role, their responses may be intentionally and appropriately misleading, in order to protect the secrecy of Pueblo religion. One Pueblo consultant said that Edward Dozier had not been initiated into the kiva, or ceremonial, society, and "he didn't have any obligations" (Pueblo interview, September 28, 1990).

In fact no firm evidence exists about whether he was initiated as a youth or whether he participated in Pueblo rituals except as an observer in public activities such as dances. The precise extent of his religious knowledge and his participation in the ceremonial life of Santa Clara Pueblo may never be known, although his letters suggest that he had no detailed personal knowledge of ceremonial activities. His siblings, however, participated in general community life in various ways. Several older brothers and sisters danced in ceremonies on the Winter side; Tom Dozier became the tribal forester; and Mike Dozier served as an elected officer (secretary) in tribal government in the late 1930s.

Whatever his ceremonial status, Dozier's legacy from his mother—the Tewa and Spanish languages, tribal membership, her Pueblo relatives, religion, clan, moiety, and political faction, and the right to inherit Pueblo property, including land—grounded him in Santa Clara culture and kinship. His father's legacy—the English language, the education Edward received, Thomas's avocational interest in ethnology and linguistics, and Edward's United States citizenship—both enabled and motivated him to expand his networks and interests later in life. His boyhood in northern New Mexico gave him knowledge of Anglo, Hispanic, and Pueblo customs and languages, a foundation that would later allow him to cross cultural borders with some ease. His complex cultural identity cannot be understood through the nineteenth-century literary stereotype of the acculturated Indian as "caught between two worlds." Rather than being a matter of polarities, his multicultural heritage was a layering of rights and responsibilities. It was pluralistic and inclusive.

Edward Dozier was fortunate to have lived at a time when federal Indian policies were changing from models of assimilation to models of self-governance. The range of possibilities created by the political, economic, and educational reforms of the Indian New Deal offered him new opportunities to choose his own path—with help from others along the way.

3

A Linguistic Path to Anthropology

Edward Dozier once remarked that... Native Americans entering the discipline often viewed anthropology as "a means to help our people."
—Beatrice Medicine, "Anthropologists and
American Indian Studies Programs"

After graduating from high school in 1935, Edward Dozier made plans to attend the University of New Mexico (UNM) in Albuquerque. His motivation to continue his education sprang partly from the life and letters of his late father, Thomas S. Dozier. Thomas had left an archive of correspondence, clippings, manuscripts, and business papers—a legacy of aspirations and accomplishments filled with fatherly advice to his children. As Edward transcribed his father's letters by typewriter in the 1930s, he searched for a role model. A relative recalled that he "was always fascinated by letters. And through the letters, finding out that his father was a very respected person that the government used to go out and consult with him about legal matters and so on . . . it gave him the sense that he could do it" (Dozier family interview, July 14, 1990).

Although his father's letters may have given Edward growing confidence, he was, like so many other beginning college students, uncertain precisely what he wanted to study. According to one of his mentors, he struck out on a path to realize his father's "ambitions, never fulfilled, because of family cares, to be a writer, in the field of the Indian" (EPD3.4, 55). But when Edward corresponded with his father's sister about his educational goals, he wrote, "I am going to try for a teacher's Certificate and then probably go into the government Service as father did" (EPD2.2, Dozier to Aunt Molly, July 11, 1935). An unidentified correspondent during the late 1930s stated that Edward wanted to become a physician or a historian or to work in forestry (EPD2.4, E.S. Lamb to Alder, July 13, 1939).

When he actually enrolled in the fall, he declared biology as his major and history as his minor. His motivation for majoring in biology is unclear. His older brother David was attending New Mexico State University in Las Cruces and studying agriculture in the hope of becoming a government extension agent (he received his BA in 1938); perhaps Edward was influenced by his example. Overall it seems more likely that a special field project on which Dozier worked during the summer of 1935—and the new mentor and life-long friend it brought him—aroused an interest in natural science.

That mentor and friend was Elizabeth Shepley Sergeant (1881–1965), a well-educated Bostonian and widely traveled literary biographer based in New York. A graduate of Bryn Mawr College in 1903, Sergeant had worked as a journalist for the *New Republic* in France during World War I. She came to the Southwest in the 1920s on the advice of her physician, in order to rehabilitate from a leg injury sustained during a war correspondents' tour of a French battlefield. In 1922 she entered Indian affairs as a political activist working on behalf of the Pueblo Indians to oppose the land-grab policies of the Bursum Bill, federal legislation that would have authorized the allotment of Pueblo land had it passed.

Like other advocates for American Indians in the 1920s and 1930s, Sergeant was a colleague and personal friend of John Collier, the commissioner of Indian affairs, and an active member of voluntary associations such as the New Mexico Association on Indian Affairs and the Eastern Association on Indian Affairs (which later merged into Oliver La Farge's Association on American Indian Affairs). She was an antimodernist who saw a need to preserve traditional lifeways in a world of rapid industrial change. Accordingly, she had been an original founder of the Indian Arts

Fund in Santa Fe, dedicated to preserving traditional Pueblo pottery (Dauber 1990). She applied her investigative and writing skills to the national issues of federal Indian policy reform, both as a self-employed writer and as a temporary government employee. From 1934 through 1936, her Pueblo field studies, her report for a federal project called the Tewa Basin Study (Sergeant 1935), and her frank manner helped Collier inform policy makers about actual conditions on reservations and aid tribes in writing constitutions under the Indian Reorganization Act.

In the summer of 1935 the BIA employed Elizabeth Sergeant as a community fieldworker to help Santa Clara leaders reorganize their government through a written constitution and bylaws. At the same time she planned and personally funded what she called the Pueblo Wild Flower Project. Although it was never completed, this ethnobotanical venture was designed to produce a book about native wildflowers as a bicultural collaboration "with Indians as contributor and collaborator." The aim of the cross-cultural project was to give "the point of view of the white Botanist and the Indian herb man" and to "reach some conception of how Indian Botany differs from white Botany" (EPD3.4, 3, 58). It was also intended to be intergenerational, with elders and young people from Santa Clara Pueblo and Tesuque Pueblo participating. Sergeant believed that contemporary Pueblo youths "needed to keep a firm footing in their old culture in order not to lose their way in the modern world" (EPD3.4, 4, 6, 58).

Thanks to Dozier's knowledge of both Tewa and English, the BIA, through its regional office, the United Pueblos Agency, hired him as interpreter and clerical assistant for Sergeant's coordination efforts on the constitution. In addition, he was one of the "educated" young Pueblos she personally employed on the Wild Flower Project "to record their own cultural materials in written as well as in pictorial form; and so far as possible in their own language" (EPD3.4, January 31, 1937). Edward had taken science in high school but was unfamiliar with scientific botany. He could, however, provide basic cultural knowledge about wildflowers that were unknown to Sergeant and her white botanist colleague, Marian Shevky. For whatever he did not know himself, he could ask his uncle (his mother's half-brother) Vidal Gutierrez, who knew the traditional medicinal uses of native plants (EPD3.4, 2; La Farge 1966).

Sergeant and Dozier became friends, and she assumed the role of mentor to her young assistant. She described him as

> a good interpreter, an unusually good typist for an Indian, and a pearl of boys in his steadiness, conscience, and serious devotion to his work. His rare objective interest in "Indian research" came quickly to light.... He became vitally interested in the plan for the Flower book, which was just taking shape. I asked him to become an Indian collaborator, and told him he should share in potential but unlikely royalties. His Uncle gave us some (free) information about the flowers, and Edward became interested, at once, in finding some method of writing his native Tewa which an Indian could grasp and practise. (EPD3.4, 57)

Elizabeth Sergeant was thirty-five years Edward's elder and, coincidentally, shared his birth date of April 23. Their friendship, similar to that between an aunt and a nephew, lasted thirty years. She expressed her encouragement of Dozier in a long correspondence that began in the 1930s and ran throughout most of his professional career. Upon her death in 1965, she willed him her Pueblo research materials, which he used in writing several articles on factionalism and governance.

It was the Wild Flower Project that introduced Dozier to the scholarly orthography of the Tewa language. A way of writing Tewa was central to publishing a book on native wildflowers in which indigenous names were to be included along with each plant's common and botanical names. As the project continued—Edward worked for Sergeant again in the summer of 1936—he struggled to teach himself formal linguistics by studying a Smithsonian booklet on the phonetic transcription of Indian languages and a publication on Tewa by the linguist John P. Harrington, a friend and associate of his father's (Harrington 1910). He was frustrated when he tried to apply anthropological linguistics and his native knowledge of Tewa to plant names. Complaining to Sergeant, he wrote that "it is hardly possible for me to give you the correct spelling and diacritical marks of Tewa words I do not hear pronounced myself" (EPD3.1, Dozier to Sergeant, January 11, 1937).

With the help of others, Dozier "worked on a simplified system of writing the Tewa language" (EPD2.3, September 25, 1936). In a compromise between scholarly linguistics and practicality, Sergeant ultimately selected the Tewa orthography of the anthropologist and writer Oliver La Farge, a friend of the Dozier family and a colleague of Sergeant's and Collier's who facilitated the Hopi constitution in 1936. This hybrid method was intended to reach an audience of "Pueblo youth" and an "average white reader of the book" (EPD3.4, 10).

The Pueblo Wild Flower Project introduced Dozier to linguistics and made him aware of the complexity of a scholarly study of the Tewa language (EPD2.3, Dozier diary, September 8, 1936). Years later, after Sergeant had died and bequeathed her research files to him, he recalled the project to the ethnobotanist Volney Jones: "I served as an interpreter for Miss Sergeant—I had not at the time either training or even a deep interest in anthropology, unfortunately" (EPD4.1, Dozier to Jones, November 1, 1965).

In retrospect, it was Dozier's knowledge of the Tewa language that paved the path to his university study of anthropology. His father had embraced an avocational interest in the tonal aspects of the Tewa language that might indirectly, through the unpublished writings that his son preserved, have encouraged Edward toward a career in anthropological linguistics. Thomas Dozier had described the tonality of Tewa this way:

> In learning any language close attention is necessary to be given to the accent. But in this Tegua the inflection of the voice is very important. . . . As an example, one asking an Indian of the Teguas his term for the moon would write *Po* (long *o*). He would necessarily write the same combination

of letters for water, except that he would have to indicate a slight explosive sound in the *p* of the latter word, and in the former he would have to indicate a rising. (EPD1.4, T.S. Dozier, "The Language of the Teguas," n.d.)

Thomas Dozier had advised that "all true ethnological research must begin with that language as the basis of enquiry" (EPD1.1, T.S. Dozier, 23 March 1894). He explained: "The medium of the spoken tongue appears to me as the surest means of obtaining a proper estimate of a people and may draw aside the veil and give us at least a partial glimpse of their past" (EPD1.1, T.S. Dozier to Crandall, May 22, 1906). Perhaps, together with the support of Elizabeth Shepley Sergeant and the Pueblo Wild Flower Project, those words helped put Edward Dozier on the path to anthropology.

That path, however, was neither straight nor smooth. During his first year at the University of New Mexico—as one of approximately a dozen American Indian students who enrolled that fall—Dozier was uncertain of his career goals. In November 1935 he wrote to Sergeant, using her as a sounding board about pursuing a course toward American Indian history and culture:

> I have been thinking lately over the choice of my life work.... Do you know if there are positions for historical research workers among the American Indians in the Indian Service? Don't you think that such workers would be valuable to our country? They may find things in the way of . . . social organizations which would be of benefit to our civilization. But the greater benefit would be rendered to the Indians themselves as defects found will be repaired.
>
> I have also thought that the government may establish a school of historical research . . . something like the art school in Santa Fe, but devoted entirely to teaching Indian history and culture. Such a school will preserve Indian culture and will make Indians realize the value of Indian things. (EPD3.1, Dozier to Sergeant, November 25, 1935)

Writing to a local BIA official, Dozier again expressed uncertainty about his major: "My vocational objective when I entered the University of New Mexico this fall was that of a government school teacher in elementary schools. But I have discovered after four months that . . . I have a greater interest . . . in historical subjects, especially in what concerns the American Indians" (EPD2.4, Dozier to E. Pierce, December 17, 1935). Nevertheless, he continued to pursue a degree in biology through 1941, meanwhile adding courses in the history of the Americas, New Mexico, and modern Europe.

Paying for higher education was a tremendous challenge for American Indian students in the early twentieth century, particularly during the Great Depression. Fortunately, Dozier was able to fund his college education partly through the generous support of his brothers and sisters and partly through seasonal government wage work. In the summer of 1936, for example, besides working for Sergeant on her wildflower project, he was hired as a file clerk and typist at the United Pueblos Agency in Albuquerque under the Indian Emergency Conservation Work program, which provided employment for American Indians in public works projects.

More importantly, Dozier was able to take advantage of timely federal programs through section 11 of the Wheeler-Howard Act of 1934, which had authorized a government-sponsored program under which loans could be made to Indian students for college tuition and related expenses. As an enrolled member of an Indian tribe, Dozier was eligible for reimbursable loans to cover his university expenses for the years 1935–37 and 1939–41. The $150 per academic year paid for tuition, books, and supplies (EPD2.4, Dozier to Bronson, April 23, 1936). In addition to attending college, however, the loan program required him to work fourteen hours every week at the U.S. Indian School in Albuquerque, where he boarded, some four miles from the university (EPD 3.1, Dozier to Sergeant, September 17, 1935). He soon became distracted in the noisy boarding school environment, and his studies suffered. Indeed, he found the university curriculum itself a challenge.

Dozier's school records reveal that during his first year at UNM he received failing grades in biology, English, and history. By January 1936 he was on probation (UNM, Office of Admissions and Records, Edward Dozier file). His poor grades from 1935 through 1937 threatened his federal loan as well. Although Dozier believed he had the intellectual capacity for college, he had to justify himself to the guidance officer at the Office of Indian Affairs in Washington, DC:

> The past school year has been my first year in a boarding school. I was not accustomed to studying in the ordinary din and bustle which is the lot of all boarding schools. . . . I spent the greater part of my time in the Indian School and associated more with its students that I at times feel that I attended the Albuquerque Indian School instead of the University. . . . I believe that if I were more interested in the University than the Indian School I would have done much better in my grades. (EPD2.4, Dozier to Bronson, July 10, 1936)

Dozier petitioned for additional loans and promised to improve his grades the following year. The government granted him a loan for a second year at UNM. Sophie Aberle, superintendent of the United Pueblos Agency, wrote a letter of support to the guidance officer, saying, "We believe he realizes fully the mistakes he made this past year and that he will make an effort to improve his work if given another chance" (EDP2.4, Aberle to Bronson, July 31, 1936).

A noteworthy event took place at Santa Clara Pueblo during Edward's first year at UNM. On January 4, 1936, he and his brother David voted by absentee ballot in the pueblo's first election of tribal officers. This was a direct result of Santa Clara's new tribal constitution, with which Edward (and David as well) had been involved through his work with Elizabeth Sergeant. As the pueblo's first written code of law, the political charter created an annual popular election for tribal officials in which any member over the age of eighteen was eligible to vote. Although nineteen-year-old

Edward was ineligible to vote on the adoption of the constitution itself, which required a voter to be twenty-one, he proudly voted for the first slate of candidates for tribal office. Coincidentally, the first elected governor under the IRA constitution, Agapito Naranjo, was from his own Winter side.

Another benefit of the Wheeler-Howard Act came to Dozier and his family not long afterward. Section 5 of the act promoted Indian tribes' acquisition of land to consolidate reservation holdings. In response, Santa Clara Pueblo purchased a small amount of additional land and distributed it through a lottery system. Dozier family members were awarded acreage at the southern boundary of the reservation, near the butte known as Black Mesa ("the lower place" in Tewa), sometime in the late 1930s. Edward received a half-acre lot, although he never used it and eventually sold the use rights to his brother Mike, who lived at the pueblo. Presumably Edward used this small income to help pay for his schooling.

By 1938 Dozier was feeling the need for a respite from college life—and from his struggle with his grades, which he described as "far from being high" (EPD3.1, Dozier to Sergeant, Fall 1935). For the first time he looked for government wage work away from his home state, and again he benefited from a provision in the Indian Reorganization Act. Section 12 authorized a hiring preference for American Indians in BIA jobs, including an exemption from Civil Service laws. Dozier successfully applied for a nine-month position as an "Indian assistant" in Washington, DC. Consequently, from November 1938 to August 1939 he worked as a mail and filing clerk in the construction division at the BIA office in the nation's capital.

Away from the pueblo and rural life in New Mexico, he grew more confident as he interacted with diverse people in the cosmopolitan capital city. He remarked a few years later, in a diary that he kept during his military service, that his physical appearance and knowledge of Spanish often caused people to take him "for a Mexican or a Latin" (EPD2.6, army diary, ca. 1943). Traveling far from the Southwest, first to Washington and later to many other places during World War II, caused Dozier to pause and reconsider his ethnic identity and the effects of racial stereotypes. He later recollected:

> An Indian in New Mexico suffers ridicule, exclusion, and abuse from the intolerant Mexican and Anglo on one hand and pampering and treatment as a museum specimen on the other hand by the curious tourist and idealistic govt Anglo employee....
>
> I am not ashamed of being an Indian—far from it. But I do not like to be treated as a subordinate because I am an Indian, nor do I like the remark of people that the Indians have advantages of education and of livelihood that whites do not have because of Govt aid. My life in the East, although I worked for the govt. (perhaps there is something to advantages referred to above) was of tremendous help. Although I worked in an Indian office my acquaintances were not Indian and for the first time I was among people who knew practically nothing about Indians, in fact I was not even taken for an Indian. This was fine because I could compete equally with them and not be pointed out as "different." (EPD2.6, army diary, ca. 1943)

In September 1939 a more self-assured Dozier returned to UNM. Immediately his grades began to improve. Although he did poorly in math, he was now earning Bs and Cs in most of his course work—zoology, botany, bacteriology, comparative plant morphology, and animal physiology. He received his first collegiate A in ethnobiology (UNM, Office of Admissions and Records, Edward Dozier file).

His return to school after the Washington job also marked a shift in his academic interests. His path was now turning increasingly toward anthropology. During the 1940–41 academic year he enrolled in three anthropology classes—two general courses and one on the anthropology of the American Indian.

Much of the credit for inspiring Dozier's interest in anthropology belonged to his professor W.W. (Nibs) Hill, who had been hired by the anthropology department at UNM in 1937. Hill, a student of the eminent linguist Edward Sapir, had received his doctorate from Yale University in 1934 with a research specialty in Navajo studies (Lange 1976:97). He came to UNM at a time when members of the Department of Anthropology were focusing their research on regional Southwestern studies (Bock 1989).

Hill's uncle, the anthropologist Matthew Sterling, who worked at the Bureau of American Ethnology, sent him an eighty-three-page unpublished manuscript on Santa Clara Pueblo written by Jean Allard Jeançon (Jeançon 1931) and asked him to complete it (Hill 1982). During the 1940–41 academic year, Hill hired Dozier as a student assistant to help him do additional ethnographic fieldwork and prepare a revised manuscript for publication. Edward worked on the project part-time (EPD3.1, Dozier to Sergeant, November 10, 1948). He was paid by the National Youth Administration, a federal program, which provided funding until he became ineligible at the age of twenty-five in 1941. Once again it was his ability as a native interpreter that qualified him for the job, and a federal government program that provided the funding.

Hill aroused his native student's interest in anthropology and in academic study generally. Dozier wrote: "Since I have been working for Dr. Hill I have changed my attitude. In fact I have even decided to take a minor in Anthropology along with a minor in History and a major in Biology. Fortunately there are some anthropologists who are interested in Indians not only to portray them idealistically and get information out of them but also because they are human beings and want to better their lives" (EPD3.1, Dozier to Sergeant, December 31, 1940).

Dozier admired Hill's fieldwork methods. Unlike some other Southwestern anthropologists, Hill shared anthropological information with the members of the village he studied. Dozier wrote to Sergeant about his job and the research at his pueblo:

> I have therefore, a part-time N.Y.A. job which is helping me greatly... I learned from a friend that Dr. W.W. Hill... had gotten hold of a Santa Clara manuscript and needed an

interpreter. I applied and was given the job. . . . I have introduced him to various people in the pueblo and we are all busy now getting information on all subjects. Dr. Hill's approach to getting information is different from other ethnologists. Formerly ethnologists did not reveal to the Indians their purpose for wanting information, in many cases they even attempted to conceal books on Indians, particularly of religion, from the Indians. I have always thought that the Indians should know and have copies of articles written about them, and I was glad to find a like opinion in Dr. Hill. (EPD3.1, Dozier to Sergeant, December 31, 1940)

But Dozier also experienced firsthand the negative reaction of a Pueblo traditionalist to published accounts of secret Pueblo ritual knowledge. Hill reported a stern verbal warning that Dozier received from a Santa Clara elder:

During the course of the fieldwork, the author had occasion to show a conservative informant, heir apparent at that time to the Winter caciqueship, a copy of Parsons's *Social Organization of the Tewa*. This resulted in one of the few instances of overt anger I witnessed in an adult. The informant vilified Parsons's informant. He then lectured the interpreter [Dozier] on the danger and disadvantages of allowing information except on the most mundane things to be divulged to outsiders. He finished this tirade by pointing out the consequences of such acts in terms of jeopardizing the well-being of the village, and then by reciting the concluding statement given at a kachina performance: "Hide it in your crotch, under your arm pits, etc." (Hill 1982:143)

Although Jeançon's manuscript and Hill's subsequent book did discuss Pueblo ritual life, it was not the main focus of Hill and Dozier's research. In any case, both teacher and student got their information about Pueblo religion from published anthropological accounts; Dozier himself apparently had little knowledge of ceremonial activities and therefore could not have revealed privileged information. Dozier wrote that he and Hill "had a fair idea of the structure of S.C. religion before we started," and "we did not touch the songs at all—there is some tie-up between songs and religion" (EPD3.1, Dozier to Sergeant, ca. 1940s). He described their careful field methods:

> We approached religion lastly when interviewing an informant, discussing agricultural implements, weaving implements, and other items of material culture and their usage and then gradually grading into discussion of religious objects and ritual. In religious interrogation we proceeded in a manner that necessitated the minimum of discussion—a single answer negative or affirmative, or in most cases complied by a mere nodding of the head. For example we would ask: In San Juan upon death of the cacique the right hand man becomes the cacique, is that true of Santa Clara? (EPD3.1, Dozier to Sergeant, ca. 1940s)

General ethnographic data came from several sources. In addition to interviewing both Summer and Winter people at Santa Clara Pueblo, Hill and Dozier drew on published anthropological accounts and on Dozier's "own life experiences as well" (EPD3.1, Dozier to Sergeant, ca. 1940s). Writing to a prospective employer in Mexico in 1951, Dozier described himself as a tribal member who had "acted as an informant and interpreter for Dr. Hill and in return gained considerable experience and training" (EPD4.1, Dozier to Noval, June 5, 1951). However, in an obituary for Hill after his death in 1976, Charles H. Lange—who eventually brought the Santa Clara ethnography to publication in 1982—remembered Dozier as "reluctant to assume any major role as informant himself" (Lange 1976:87). These contradictory statements leave a sense of ambiguity about his role as facilitator or informant in Hill's field study. With his limited cultural knowledge, it is probable that any information he provided was more sociological than ethnological.

In the summer of 1941 Dozier was planning to attend UNM's linguistics field school in Chaco Canyon, New Mexico, where he would "learn transcribing from Dr. [Harry] Hoijer, and give some time as a linguistic informant for our students" (EPD4.1, Spier to Dozier, May 8, 1941). It was going to be Edward's first opportunity to learn how "to write the Tewa dialect" from Hoijer, a professional linguist who had been trained by Edward Sapir (EPD3.1, Dozier to Sergeant, April 20, 1941). World War II interrupted his plans. His draft board would not allow him to complete the last fifteen semester hours required for his baccalaureate degree (EPD2.6, Dozier memo to Intelligence Officer, Chico Army Flying School, April 5, 1943). Dozier explained to his professor Leslie Spier: "I will not be able to come to Chaco.... The Draft Board did not grant me a deferment and my induction papers are due any day.... I have enlisted in the Army Air Corps" (EPD4.1, Dozier to Spier, August 7, 1941).

Military service changed Dozier's life just as it did the lives of thousands of other American Indians between 1941 and 1945. Army life offered American Indians an equal and fair chance to compete with others for advancement, and in time Dozier became a staff sergeant. With his preference for office and clerical work, he tried to apply to the intelligence schools, but he did not qualify because, ironically, he lacked the required foreign language competency (EPD3.1, Dozier to Sergeant, ca. early 1940s). Yet he progressed in other arenas. Dozier confided in his diary:

> In the Army, I have made tremendous strides in strengthening my self-confidence.... It gave me considerable pleasure to pass an interviewing board of 6 officers for Officer's Candidate a short time ago.
>
> There is of course still abundant evidence of my inadequate background. My speech still carries trace of an Indian accent and I become greatly disturbed when I must speak for any length of time but on the whole life among whites has dispelled largely my self-consciousness. (EPD2.6, army diary, ca. 1943)

Figure 3. Edward Dozier in the Army Air Corps, 1941. During World War II Dozier enlisted and served four years of active duty. He advanced in rank from private to staff sergeant and served in the 873rd Squadron, 498th Bombardment Group, on Saipan Island, Mariana Islands, Micronesia. He was honorably discharged in November 1945. (Photograph courtesy of the Dozier family)

As part of his emerging sense of self during wartime, he Americanized his Spanish baptismal name, Eduardo de Pasqual Dozier, to Edward P. Dozier. In July 1943, during a furlough, he married Claire Elizabeth (Betty) Butler, a young Anglo woman whom he had met and dated in Washington, DC, while he clerked at the BIA office in 1938–39. Betty had attended Strayer's Secretarial School and held a clerical job at the Library of Congress. The two had met while living in the same boardinghouse and had stayed in touch over the years. In April 1944, while Edward was overseas with the Army Air Corps, Betty gave birth to a daughter, Wanda.

Dozier traveled widely for training as a clerk and on assignments involving cryptographic systems for the Intelligence Office during World War II—to California, Missouri, Colorado, Utah, Nebraska, Kansas, and the Pacific Islands. During his year of duty at Camp Susupe, a U.S. naval station on Saipan in the Mariana Islands in 1944–45, Dozier pursued an ethnographic interest in the Chamorro people who lived there. W.W. Hill encouraged him, writing that "almost nothing has been done on your particular island" (EPD4.1, Hill to Dozier, December 28, 1944). He asked Dozier to send him carbon copies of his field notes, for security's sake. Dozier secured a pass to Charankanoa village "for the purpose of making a social study"; it was his intention to "submit [it] to the University for additional credit toward a degree in Anthropology" (EPD2.6, Dozier to Lt. Col. De Witt, June 29, 1945).

Dozier managed to follow his linguistic interests, too, while in the military. He had a copy of the "English-Chamorro Primer" prepared by the education office of the military government section at Saipan, and he was learning Japanese at the base. Although Dozier described his Spanish language skills as "rusty," he was able to confer with local Catholic missionaries who had translated the Bible into the Chamorro language. He kept the information he collected in a small field journal. He also observed firsthand the social dynamics at the local civilian internment camp, where Korean and Japanese inmates were confined to fenced areas and guarded by Chamorros (EPD2.6, Saipan journal, July 6, 1945). Although Dozier never published his ethnographic descriptions of Saipan, his experience of observing culture contacts during wartime left a lasting impression. Years later, in 1959–60, he would return to the Pacific as a university ethnologist to conduct a scholarly study of the Kalinga people of northern Luzon in the Philippines (Dozier 1966b, 1967a).

On October 19, 1945, Edward Dozier was honorably discharged with the rank of staff sergeant (NARA, National Personnel Records Center, St. Louis, Edward Dozier file). Joining his wife and seventeen-month-old daughter, he came home to Santa Clara to live in his mother's house. He worked for a while at nearby Los Alamos National Laboratories, along with many other local Pueblo people. He could see that great changes had been set in motion by the return of so many Pueblo veterans. By April 1944, forty-two Santa Clara men and women, including Edward's brothers Mike and Tom, had been in the armed services (NARA, RG 75, UPA, war records for Santa Clara Pueblo, 1943–45, RM). Dozier must have foreseen these changes long before the war ended, because Hill wrote to his former assistant in June 1943: "I think that you are dead right when you say a big change is in the making at Santa Clara. A tenth of the population in the army cannot fail to leave its mark especially as the older gang will probably pass out of the picture before the fellows get back" (EPD4.1, Hill to Dozier, June 15, 1943).

Before war's end, Dozier had begun to write about assimilation, too—his belief that American Indians would be "merged with the white race in a matter of a few years and I really see no harm in it" (EPD2.6, army diary, ca. 1943). He respected "old Indian life," he said, but saw that cultural traditions and tribal cohesion were diminishing quickly. Dozier had supported the political changes brought by the 1935 constitution at his home village, and even before the war he had written to Sergeant about the "need for a separation of religion from government":

> Moiety and "old customs" party affiliations have been replaced by purely political alignments. Even in some of the dances, formerly belonging to one moiety, members of

both moieties take part—preserving the dance not in the old religious sense, but as an art form. But my ethnologist friends are greatly disturbed! They are jealous for progress among their own people, yet among the pueblos they want to perpetuate a cacique dictatorship. I cannot understand this. (EPD3.1, Dozier to Sergeant, December 31, 1940)

In the same letter he expressed the belief that Indian religion would not appeal to an "Indian who has been exposed to white civilization other than as beautiful art and ritualism."

Consequently, salvage ethnography seemed to him the best course for preserving what remained of Pueblo culture. In a letter to Sergeant written sometime in the early 1940s he said:

As to my work in Ethnology at Santa Clara: Dr. W.W. Hill and I worked for about a year, off and on.... I believe that in that time we recorded the root of what is left of Santa Clara religion (ritual) and much of the material culture.... I believe that we nipped Santa Clara just in time—I feel that cultural disintegration will come fast now, especially with the war. Perhaps because of this inevitability and realization of it that Santa Clarans were not so reluctant to disclose what they knew. But there is much that can be done in Santa Clara and other villages; the old ones who know are going, but the new ones are more accessible and there are many who possess curious minds and wish to record. (EPD3.1, Dozier to Sergeant, ca. early 1940s)

In his army diary he expressed a similar sentiment: "I am all for preserving in print what is left of the culture and feel that all those who have knowledge of it should be encouraged to record it before it disappears" (EPD2.6, Dozier army diary, ca. 1943).

Dozier's military experience only intensified his interest in anthropology. An article written about him some years later explained: "It took a war year on the island of Saipan, where he saw the impact of troop movements on a minority culture at first hand, to shift his intellectual interests from biology, his undergraduate major, to anthropology" (*Newsweek* 1952:67). In the spring semester of 1946, Dozier returned to UNM as a veteran on the GI Bill and changed his major to anthropology.

He also recaptured his interest in studying the Tewa language. He took two linguistics classes—a problems class in the analysis of the Tewa language from Leslie Spier and a course in field research on the Tewa language from Paul Reiter. Overcoming his bashfulness, he asked to give a lecture on "his people" to Florence Hawley Ellis's ethnography class and "did an excellent job" (Florence Hawley Ellis, interview, October 10, 1990).

In August 1946 Dozier and his wife, Betty, decided to separate. They both moved to Albuquerque, Edward to enroll at UNM and Betty to work. Wanda stayed on at Santa Clara with her Pueblo relatives for a while. There she was quickly "building up a vocabulary in both Tewa and English" (EPD2.2, Dozier to Leocadia Dozier, February 10, 1947). The Doziers' divorce was formalized two years later, and mother and daughter moved back to Washington, DC, where they lived with Betty's mother until Wanda was about four. Then, by verbal agreement, Edward and Betty sent Wanda to Santa Clara to live with her Tewa aunts and uncles until she was seven, when she was to be educated outside the pueblo.

Edward Dozier was awarded his bachelor of arts degree in anthropology on June 7, 1947, and immediately enrolled in graduate school at UNM. For his master's thesis he chose the topic "A Tentative Description and Classification of Tewa Verb Structure" (Dozier 1949). Backed by his committee—Florence Hawley Ellis, H.G. Alexander, Paul Reiter, and chairman W.W. Hill—Dozier began a challenging linguistic study of Santa Clara Tewa, a tonal language in the Kiowa-Tanoan language family and one of several dialects of Tewa spoken in the six northern Rio Grande Pueblos (San Juan, Santa Clara, San Ildefonso, Nambe, Pojoaque, and Tesuque).

In keeping with the academic training he had received from his UNM professors—including visiting professor Harry Hoijer, who had returned to the University of California at Los Angeles—Dozier took a Boasian approach and collected descriptive data on Tewa grammar for "historical reconstructive" purposes (Dozier

1949:33). Following the model of Hoijer's many studies of Apachean verb structure (see Bright 1964), Dozier chose the structure (morphology) of Tewa verbs as his topic. He found that each Tewa verb possessed a base consisting of a pronoun complex and a verb theme, followed by a "final verb stem." In this structure, "pronouns occur prefixed to verbs, stems are compounded, and tense-modal elements [are] suffixed" (Dozier 1949:2). He noted that pronouns were probably "the most difficult of Tewa grammatical elements to explain and classify . . . [because] the speaker of Tewa is enabled to make subtle and complicated distinctions in defining subject-object relationships" (Dozier 1949:18).

Theoretically, Dozier, as a student linguist, was committed to contemporary concepts of language and culture studies. In his thesis he concluded that Tewa tense-modal elements "promise to give insights into concepts of time, matter, duration, intensity and the like of a radically different nature from those common in the Western world" (Dozier 1949:17). Like other thesis writers, he argued that his topic had never before been adequately studied: "Linguistic material published to date is that of one authority, John P. Harrington. Almost all of this material was gathered and published between the years 1905 and 1915. A complete phonological and grammatical description of Tewa does not exist" (Dozier 1949:5).

But Dozier brought something new to the academic study of American Indian languages—the perspective of someone who was simultaneously an anthropologist and an American Indian. He positioned himself as an indigenous scholar, "a native speaker of Tewa" (Dozier 1949:3), and a young anthropologist. As a master's candidate at UNM, he was already keenly aware of academic concerns about scientific objectivity. He recognized the need to reassure his professors that he had not relied solely on his own knowledge but had collected linguistic data from a broader sample of Tewa speakers. In the abstract to his master's thesis he explained: "The major portion of the linguistic material examined is that of the writer's native dialect, Tewa. This study, however, is not based on this one source of the material alone. Paradigms and texts from other native speakers have been recorded and studied in order to supplement the materials and to insure [sic] the validity of the conclusions reached" (Dozier 1949:n.p.). In the introduction he reemphasized his objectivity: "Particular pains have been taken in this study to examine and test out every analysis. To provide a check on the validity of the writer's conclusions, a substantial number of randomly selected verb constructions have been incorporated into this study" (Dozier 1949:34).

It was appropriate not only from an academic perspective but also from a cultural one for Dozier to situate himself as just one individual speaker within a larger social network of Tewa language speakers. Pueblo people value language as cultural property —it belongs to no one person but is vested in the community at large. Spoken language is the primary means by which Pueblos express and preserve their traditional culture. As a member of a Pueblo community, Dozier was conforming to this cultural value in the way he presented himself in his thesis.

As an indigenous anthropologist, Dozier had dual responsibilities to his academic and cultural communities. His role as an anthropologist required him to employ standard linguistic field methods and analyses despite his native knowledge of Tewa. As a student anthropologist, he had to distance himself from the studied community (which problematically included himself), comply with the scientific tenets of objectivity, and write an individual, authoritative thesis on the Tewa language. At the same time, he was careful to defer to other Tewa speakers—his informants—as members of a corporate community possessing linguistic knowledge. He was carefully creating the appropriate objective distance as an anthropologist while retaining his indigenous solidarity as a Pueblo Indian.

Dozier's thesis reflected his Pueblo heritage, his university education, and the multilingual environment of northern New Mexico. Taking a generational approach to language and history, he wrote:

> Like most New Mexico Pueblos, Santa Clara speakers have passed through stages of bilingualism and trilingualism. All of the older individuals, seventy years of age and older, speak Tewa and Spanish. The next group, from about forty-five to seventy years of age, are trilingual; they speak Tewa, Spanish, and English. Individuals forty-five years of age and younger speak only Tewa and English. This interesting transition has taken place because prior to statehood (1912) New Mexico was predominantly Spanish speaking. (Dozier 1949:5–6)

It is interesting that Dozier, a thirty-three-year-old native speaker with trilingual abilities, was an exception to his own generalization.

Edward Dozier received his master's degree in anthropology at the University of New Mexico on June 6, 1949. He summarized his data on Tewa verb structure in his first linguistic publication, a paper in the *International Journal of American Linguistics* (Dozier 1953).

Although UNM was one of only a few universities at the time that offered a doctoral degree in anthropology (Bock 1989), Dozier decided not to continue his graduate work there. Instead, he moved to Los Angeles to enroll in a new doctoral program at the University of California (UCLA). His decision may have been influenced by his UNM professors, who had earned their degrees at diverse universities—Hill at Yale, Spier at Columbia, Ellis at Chicago, and Frank Hibben at Harvard (Bock 1989). Together they may have set his sights on an institution of higher learning outside of New Mexico.

Edward Dozier's native language skills and his growing interest in American Indian linguistics were continuing to lead him along the path to a career in anthropology. He credited Elizabeth Shepley Sergeant for her years of encouragement, writing that his "choice of anthropology and linguistics as a profession was made largely through her influence" (EPD4.1, Dozier to Agnes de Lima, July 7, 1965). In a letter to Sergeant, Dozier explained his doctoral plans:

I . . . am now working on a Masters—concentrating on studies with Dr. Leslie Spier. He has arranged a working scholarship at the University of California in Los Angeles for me next semester where I shall be studying linguistics with Dr. Hoijer the linguist and Mexican ethnology with Dr. Ralph Beals. . . .

I have plans to work for a Ph.D. in Anthropology and may go East to get it. At the moment Chicago, Columbia, Yale, and Harvard look equally good, however, I have a year to make up my mind. (EPD3.1, Dozier to Sergeant, April 28, 1947)

Although Dozier had been asked to come to the University of Chicago, where he knew Fred Eggan, a Southwestern ethnographer who had studied the Hopis, the better choice seemed to be UCLA, where he could work with linguist Harry Hoijer. Leslie Spier arranged for Dozier to transfer to UCLA in 1947 as an unclassified graduate student, even while he remained a master's candidate at UNM (EPD2.4, UCLA transcript, Edward Dozier). The following year he began work as Hoijer's teaching assistant, and in 1949 he officially enrolled in UCLA's new doctoral program. There, his trilingual competence and his keen interest in Tewa linguistics would guide him toward a dissertation project that was particularly suited to a Pueblo Indian and an anthropologist.

4

Fieldwork with Clan Relatives, the Arizona Tewas

It was natural for him to go out there [to Tewa Village], because of his ancestors.
— Fred Eggan, interview, May 12, 1988

Relatives of Edward Dozier's remembered that graduate school at UCLA was a challenge for him. One family member recalled: "They gave him a hard time at UCLA. They were giving all of their students a hard time. . . . It was a new department and they wanted their students to make a mark for them. . . . They wanted very, very good theoretical work to come out . . . to produce famous students" (Dozier family interview, July 13, 1990).

Even getting accepted into the program posed its difficulties. Charles H. Lange, a fellow graduate student of Dozier's at UNM, recalled:

> [Harry Hoijer] didn't think that Ed was capable of it. He thought New Mexico is one place and UCLA is another. They thought of themselves, and they were, pretty high-powered intellectuals there—Hoijer and [Walter] Goldschmidt and some of the others. So they discouraged him. . . . But then they had a linguistic exam and he turned his paper in. He was the only one who got an A in the class. He was the only one who really got to the heart of it. And Hoijer changed his attitude about him completely and said, "Ed should be my assistant and he should come to UCLA." (Charles H. Lange, interview, May 7, 1988)

Dozier enrolled at UCLA as a graduate student in anthropology in the fall semester of 1948, the year the new doctoral program was established. His classes included "Indians of Modern Mexico" and "Theory and Method" with Ralph Beals, "American Culture" with Walter Goldschmidt, and "Introduction to Linguistics" with Hoijer. Unlike at UNM, he received consistently high grades. He also gained experience as Hoijer's research assistant that first year and as his teaching assistant the second (EPD4.1, Dozier to Noval, June 5, 1951). Charles Lange speculated on the importance of anthropological linguistics at UCLA: "I think initially . . . Hoijer was looking to getting the linguistic program started and here was a built-in informant. So he made him a TA [teaching assistant] or something. All he had to do was talk Tewa so many hours a week" (Charles H. Lange, interview, May 12, 1988). Dozier also assisted Hoijer when he taught linguistics at the University of California–Berkeley in the summer of 1949. At Hoijer's invitation, Dozier participated in teaching a Tewa language course for the Linguistics Institute at the University of Michigan in Ann Arbor that summer as well. Having taken classes in philology from Hoijer at both UNM and UCLA, Dozier was well trained in the Boasian study of Native American languages.

By 1949 Hoijer and his Pueblo Indian graduate student had developed their relationship to the point of collaborating on a paper about Santa Clara Tewa phonemes (Hoijer and Dozier 1949). In it Hoijer expanded upon his study of American Indian linguistics, and Dozier contributed research on Tewa linguistics from his UNM master's thesis. Hoijer acknowledged Dozier as coauthor on the paper. When it appeared in the *International Journal of American Linguistics,* Dozier became the first published American Indian linguist of the Tewa language. He expanded the Boasian practice of acknowledging American Indian coauthors (see Norcini 1995); this time the coauthor was a native scholar with academic training in anthropological linguistics.

The Department of Anthropology at UCLA, with a faculty that could trace its intellectual genealogy to Boas and Sapir, taught the American historical tradition to a new generation of postwar graduate students. They learned that a professional anthropologist objectively described the cultural "particulars" of Native American life without attempting premature generalizations, classifications, or theoretical interpretations. Cultural elements were to be observed and recorded factually within the overall context of culture history. Elders were to be consulted to ensure the greatest temporal depth of knowledge. As social scientists, they were to collect linguistic data and traditional narratives that would reveal implicit and unconscious categories of native meaning and values.

Following in this Americanist tradition, Dozier began to plan his dissertation research, which would again be a linguistic study. With his master's degree in hand from UNM in June 1949, he was eager to follow the next step in his path toward a career in academic anthropology—the rite of passage known as "going into the field." He was now a mature thirty-three-year-old, the divorced father of a five-year-old daughter who was living at Santa Clara Pueblo with his brothers and sisters. He was a World War II veteran, well traveled, savvy about Pueblo politics, and professionally trained in anthropological research.

He chose as his research site a Pueblo community called Tewa Village, located on First Mesa on the Hopi reservation in eastern Arizona. It had formerly been called Hano, an Anglicized version of the Hopi name for the village. Hopis, outsiders, and the older generation of Hopi-Tewas still widely knew it by that name.

Tewa-speaking people from the Galisteo Basin in north-central New Mexico had founded Hano in 1696 at the invitation of the Hopi leaders during a time of turmoil following the Pueblo Revolt of 1680 and the Spanish reconquest of 1692. The Hopis gave the Tewas land and other incentives to settle on First Mesa in return for helping protect them from their surrounding enemies, the Utes and Navajos. Over the course of 250 years, the Tewas intermarried with the Hopis, became integrated into the Hopi social and ceremonial system, and served as interpreters for the Hopis with federal government (BIA) officials.

But the Hopi-Tewa people also had disagreements with the

Figure 4. Edward Dozier with his daughter Wanda at the family home in Santa Clara Pueblo, 1949. After Dozier and Betty Butler divorced in May 1948, Wanda spent some of her childhood years in the village with her father's relatives and learned to speak the Tewa language. (Photograph courtesy of the Dozier family)

Hopis over perceived mistreatment and unfulfilled promises of land. In response, the Arizona Tewas, although accommodating to some facets of Hopi cultural life, proudly preserved aspects of their independent cultural identity, particularly their language. The most obvious expression of this cultural distinctiveness was an imposed language barrier expressed in a legendary curse, about which Dozier would later write. According to this curse, the Tewas were able to speak the Hopi language and even act as their tribal interpreters, but the Hopis were disallowed from learning or speaking the Tewa language (Dozier 1954a; Kroskrity 1993). The language barrier survived even intermarriage. In Hopi-Tewa families, the Tewa spouse spoke Hopi, but the Hopi spouse did not speak Tewa.

The people of Tewa Village and nearby Polacca spoke a dialect of Tewa that was mutually intelligible with Santa Clara Tewa, although it took some effort. By selecting Tewa Village as his dissertation site, Dozier would be able to use his birthright language to advantage with his distant linguistic relatives while avoiding the complications of conducting research at his home village (Charles H. Lange, interview, May 12, 1988).

As a major component of his dissertation, Dozier planned to make a linguistic study of ancestral Tewa as spoken at Tewa Village. His hypothesis was that the Tewa speakers who had split off from the main language group in New Mexico in the late seventeenth century and lived in greater isolation on the mesa tops had consequently retained more of the ancestral way of speaking than had Rio Grande Tewas. He explained his dissertation proposal to Elizabeth Sergeant: "My Ph.d thesis is to be a comparison of Hano (Hopi Tewa) with Santa Clara—language and culture" (EPD3.1, Dozier to Sergeant, April 25, 1948).

A predoctoral fellowship from the Social Science Research Council (1949–50) and a John Hay Whitney Opportunity Fellowship (1950–51) funded Dozier's fieldwork at Hano. The Whitney fellowships provided minority candidates with opportunities for educational advancement and leadership in academia, the arts, and the humanities (Kahn 1981). In 1950 Dozier was one of the first of eighty-five American Indian scholars to receive Whitney fellowships (Raushenbush 1972:10; *Santa Fe New Mexican,* circa 1950). A grant of between $1,000 and $3,000 not only provided him with needed supplemental funding for his fieldwork but also, and more importantly, gave him national prestige and access to a network of intellectuals and philanthropists throughout his

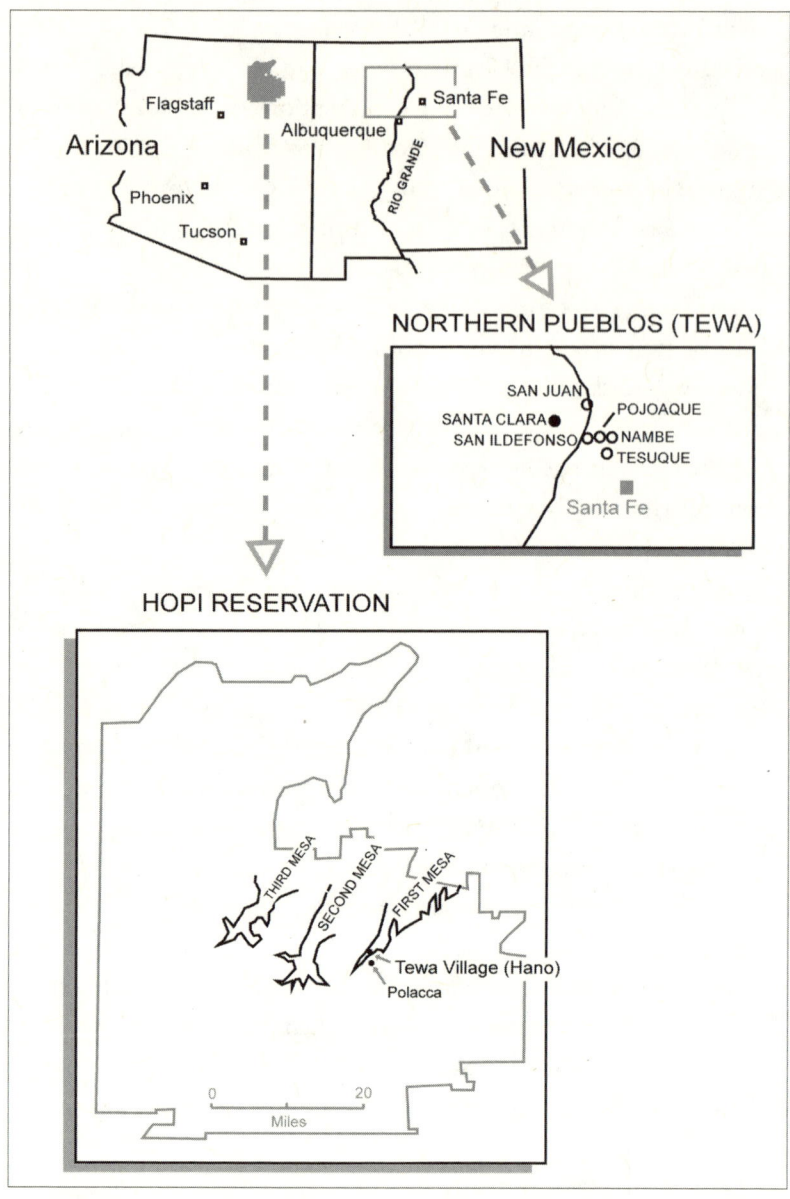

Figure 5. Dozier, born at Santa Clara Pueblo in north-central New Mexico, conducted his UCLA dissertation fieldwork at Tewa Village (Hano) on the Hopi reservation in northeastern Arizona. Kinship relationships between these two communities of Tewa language speakers were important to Dozier as a Pueblo Indian anthropologist. (Map courtesy of Philip G. Chase)

career. Between the time of Dozier's award and his death, the John Hay Whitney Opportunity Fellows included other native scholars, among them Clara Sue Kidwell (Choctaw), Edmund Ladd (Zuni), D'Arcy McNickle (Flathead-Salish), Alfonso Ortiz (San Juan Pueblo), and Robert K. Thomas (Cherokee). The scholar Vine Deloria Jr. (Standing Rock Sioux) called the Opportunity Fellowships "probably the single most influential program in Indian education in this century. All the academic leadership came out of there" (Vine Deloria Jr., interview, July 19, 1990). For Dozier, the fellowship was identification as an emerging native scholar.

With full funding, Dozier concentrated on his research at Tewa Village. He recorded his methodology, contacts, and data. He kept typed field notes from his work in 1949–50 and labeled them "Running Narrative." He may have modeled his field notes on writings made by the anthropologist Oliver La Farge in the mid-1930s to inform the commissioner of Indian affairs about progress on the Hopi constitution. La Farge, too, had called his notes "Running Narrative" (McNickle 1971:113). Dozier knew La Farge, president of the Association on American Indian Affairs and a long-time family friend, and had consulted him, along with other researchers, in compiling a list of Hopi and Anglo contacts who had facilitated prior anthropological research.

Dozier began his fieldwork at the Keams Canyon Indian Agency, not far from Tewa Village on First Mesa. There he chose at first to conceal his Indian identity. He explained why in his journal (the idiosyncratic spellings in this and subsequent quotations are Dozier's):

> I purposely did not declare myself as a Tewa Indian in my encounters with either Hopi or White individuals that I met during this day. I wanted to discouver, if possible, if I could catch the Tewa language spoken by individuals around the Agency grounds. . . . I knew that I could not possibley hide my Tewa identity beyond a day or so, for in close compact communities, news gets around fast. On this day, I was impressed with the amount of Tewa that I heard

spoken by workers and apparently residents on the Agency grounds and in the Trading Posts. (EPD4.2, Running Narrative, summer 1949:4)

Later in the day Dozier met Albert Yava (Yava 1978), the official interpreter for the Hopis, whom La Farge had mentioned as a possible contact. Dozier introduced himself in the Tewa language as a Tewa Indian. Yava was surprised. He smiled, saying, "I saw you at the Agency this morning, and I wondered what kind of an Indian you were. I didn't realize that you were of my own tribe" (Yava, in EPD4.2, Running Narrative, summer 1949:6).

After identifying himself as a Tewa, Dozier discussed his research idea with Yava and gained his support for a language study at Hano.

> I told him that I plan to do a study of the Tewa language. He was much interested in this project and told me that he was well acquinted with a linguist by the name of Edward Kennard.... I said though I did not know Kennard myself, I had heard a great deal about him from Dr. Hoijer....
>
> I told Yava that I wanted to make a study of the Tewa language and the best way to study a language was to live with the people who spoke it. (EPD4.2, Running Narrative, summer 1949:6–7)

Yava suggested that he "find an older man with whom to study . . . the orthodox Tewa language" (EPD4.2, Running Narrative, summer 1949:8). Dozier then drove his station wagon to Tewa Village and began to introduce himself. As he did, his "few words in Tewa brought forth loud exclamations" (EPD4.2, Running Narrative, summer 1949:9), and he was surrounded by people speaking Tewa. "I soon found out that though my Tewa was understandable to them after several repitions, their Tewa likewise needed repeating for me to understand them. However, a mixed English and Tewa was very effective" (EPD4.2, Running Narrative, summer 1949:9).

Not all of Dozier's conversations went smoothly. The wife of

Bert Yuvella, the Hano chief, had difficulty understanding him (EPD4.2, Running Narrative, summer 1949:10). At a farm in Wepo Wash, below First Mesa on its western edge, he and the local residents struggled to communicate. He wrote:

> I was not accoustomed to their Tewa, nor were they accoustomed to mine. However, as I had learned the morning before a mixture of English and Tewa works very well indeed. Apparently most of the Hopi Tewa had learned to converse in this fashion with their Rio Grande Tewa relatives. They seemed to catch on to my Tewa more readily than I caught on to theirs. . . . When they talked among themselves in Tewa, I could hardly understand a word they said. But when they spoke to me they spoke much slower, [replacing] some of their own peculiar terms [with] what they knew to be Rio Grande Tewa useage. (EPD4.2, Running Narrative, summer 1949:12–13)

In spite of dialect differences with Dozier, the family at Wepo Wash invited him to live with them and learn their language. He reciprocated, offering to work at their summer camp "just as long as they spoke . . . exclusively in Hopi Tewa" (EPD4.2, Running Narrative, summer 1949:13). As he described it later in his dissertation: "I said that I had studied 'languages' in college and I would like to make a study of the differences and similarities between the Tewa spoken in Santa Clara and the Tewa spoken at Tewa village. This news was received with interest and many members of the group declared themselves available for such work" (Dozier 1952:4). Accordingly, he stayed for the summer of 1949 and conducted a "preliminary survey of the Hopi-Tewa" language and culture. Because extended visits to the Hopi villages by Pueblo relatives were common, Dozier's stay during the summer of 1949 was considered a customary social visit. "I was received with considerable warmth—as any other visitor from my village would have been," he wrote (Dozier 1954a:260).

On his occasional automobile trips off the reservation that summer, he often took along his friends from Tewa Village as

Figure 6. Summer sheep camp near the Hopi mesas where Dozier lived with an Arizona Tewa family during his dissertation research in the summer of 1949. The following year he lived in a house in Polacca, where he was joined by his second wife, Marianne Fink. (Photograph courtesy of the Dozier family; Edward Dozier, photographer)

a way to reciprocate their hospitality. When he brought Santa Clarans to Tewa Village to participate in the Yandewa dance, which the Hopi-Tewas had borrowed from Santa Clara Pueblo, the guests were "feted in almost every Hopi-Tewa home" (Dozier 1952:5). Dozier observed the cordial interactions between members of the two groups and the "deep respect the Hopi-Tewa have for their linguistic kinfolk" (Dozier 1952:5).

This visit by Dozier's fellow Santa Clarans was significant in his successful fieldwork as an indigenous scholar at Tewa Village. It enhanced his kinship ties and raised his social status as a close clansman. Until this time he had possessed little to "exchange" with the Arizona Tewas, because apparently he was not, by either training or practice, a bearer of ceremonial knowledge. Bringing his Santa Clara relatives, who did have knowledge of songs and dances, to Hano gave him improved status and quickly led the Hopi-Tewas to accept him as a clan relative. He wrote that "the visit was . . . useful to me in cementing my own relations with the Hopi-Tewa, for after that visit I was regarded as a very close friend and everyone began to exchange clan relationship terms with me" (Dozier 1952:5).

Unlike the Rio Grande Tewas, who structured their social life around the moiety system, the Arizona Tewas had adapted to the Hopi principle of matrilineal clans as the foundation of social organization. Although clans existed at Santa Clara Pueblo, they had minimal reported social or ritual importance. Dozier's affiliation with his mother's Badger clan was, however, a critical element in establishing his unique field relations at Tewa Village. Clan affiliation situated Dozier physically, socially, economically, and politically within the community. The husband of his first host family at Tewa Village in 1949 belonged "to the Hopi Butterfly clan which is linked with the Badger. . . . My own clan in Santa Clara . . . is Badger," he wrote (EPD4.2, field diary, 1949). This affiliation was translated into the Arizona Tewa system of linked clans, or phratries.

Following norms of reciprocity, the Arizona Tewas extended to their Santa Clara kinsman an appropriate clan term, *memeh*, meaning "mother's elder brother" (an older man in one's own clan). Dozier was honored by this sign of respect: "At Tewa Village I was called *memeh* by the very old as well as by the very young" (Dozier 1954a:310). Although it is not uncommon for anthropologists to develop fictive kinship with their hosts during their fieldwork, Dozier was unusual in that his clan affiliation was authentic, derived from family heritage and reciprocal relations between Tewa Village and Santa Clara Pueblo.

In the summer of 1950 he began a second season of fieldwork. Now he operated out of his new residence, a government-built stone house in the predominantly Hopi-Tewa town of Polacca, below First Mesa just south of Tewa Village. By now Dozier had remarried, too. He and Marianne Fink had met at UNM in the fall or winter of 1949, introduced by a mutual friend who thought Dozier might be interested in Fink's research for a master's degree, which involved psychological testing of Navajo children. The two dated and attended several Pueblo dances. They were married in July 1950, and Marianne joined Edward at Hopi. In the more relaxed and private location of their Polacca house, he interviewed people and gathered cultural information in the Tewa language. To Dozier, his clan relatives who volunteered their assistance were more friends than informants (Dozier 1952:6).

Because he was incorporated into Hopi-Tewa life as a kinsman, Dozier found the Arizona Tewas much more forthcoming in talking to him than an anthropologist might have expected of the usually secretive Pueblos. The anthropologist Elsie Clews Parsons once called them "past masters in the art of defeating inquiry" (Parsons 1929:7). In the 1940s W.W. Hill reported that informants sometimes politely "denied knowledge of certain areas of the culture with which they were commonly recognized to be familiar. This recourse allowed them to preserve their own integrity without violating the dictates of good manners through direct refusal" (Hill 1982:141). Dozier himself quoted the anthropologist Leslie White regarding the value the Pueblos placed on secrecy: "[Pueblo] children are taught from infancy to tell outsiders nothing. Strict watch is kept over all that none may betray the pueblo's secrets" (Dozier 1955c: 194).

The Pueblos' most closely guarded secret was their ritual knowledge. A Pueblo person explained: "Usually before we go in [to the kiva] and get initiated they tell us, 'Whatever's done here, it's kept here. Don't take it out. Just leave it in the kiva'" (Pueblo interview, October 16, 1990). The anthropologist Ruth Benedict, explaining the "absence" of ritual tales at Cochiti Pueblo, wrote that it was disloyal "to tell them to the whites, even when the white friend is accepted and valued" (Benedict 1931:201).

According to acculturation theory, which was popular among anthropologists at the time and to which Dozier himself subscribed—with some significant modifications (Dozier 1961a)—secrecy was a Pueblo response to changes forced upon American

Indians by the dominant society. Some anthropologists, including Dozier (1966c), have argued that the Pueblos' reluctance to talk to outsiders was "merely a special case of a much larger [internal] process" (Brandt 1980:124). By means of secrecy, those who possessed ritual knowledge could retain it, along with its concomitant power (Brandt 1985). W.W. Hill observed at Santa Clara in the 1940s that although "in theory secretiveness applied primarily to relations with outsiders, it actually went beyond this and permeated everyday relationships within the village as well" (Hill 1982:142).

Edward Dozier had no intention of making religion a focus of his ethnography; he was too well socialized as a Pueblo Indian to do something so contrary to traditional law. His main purpose at Tewa Village was to study language. Yet even that might have posed difficulties for anyone else. Pueblos could be secretive about their languages as well, as the Hopi-Tewas' language curse attests. Some Pueblos particularly objected to having their language written down, as Dozier would be doing, believing that to write it was to make public the private knowledge of a community of speakers. One Pueblo interviewee told an old story to illustrate the ingenious ways in which the Rio Grande Tewas kept their language hidden from their Hispanic neighbors in the past:

> Ed was saying once about how at Santa Clara there is no Tewa word for horse, because horses are a Spanish introduction. So let's say there are a couple of [Hispanics] there and there's two Tewas . . . talking away. The word that they would use for horse is *cabajo,* from the Spanish *caballo.* But if there's two [Hispanics] listening there, they'd be able to pick up and say, ah, these guys are talking about horses. So what they'll say is when a [Hispanic] is listening, "I'm going over to the field to feed my big dog that eats grass." And the Tewas would know that they're talking about horses and the guys that are there would never know that they were talking about horses. (Pueblo interview, October 16, 1990)

That the Arizona Tewas eagerly approved Dozier's proposed language study may attest to the privileged relationship he enjoyed as kinsman to his hosts. Clearly, they did not include him in the category of persons from whom their language should be kept secret. He was even able to document and interpret the history of the Tewa language curse. It was told to him in their Tewa dialect, and he then translated it "as accurate as I could make it" (Dozier 1954a:292, n. 15). It was a story about how the Arizona Tewas had sealed off knowledge of their language from the Hopis after years of mistreatment and broken promises:

> Our clan chiefs dug a pit between Tewa Village and the Hopi towns and told the Hopi clan chiefs to spit into it. When they had all spat, our clan chiefs spat above the spittle of the Hopi. The pit was refilled, and then our clan chiefs declared:
>
> "Because you have behaved in a manner unbecoming to human beings, we have sealed knowledge of our language and our way of life from you. You and your descendants will never learn our language and our ceremonies, but we will learn yours. We will ridicule you in both your language and our own." (Dozier 1954a:292, n. 15, 16)

This symbolic moment in the preservation of the Arizona Tewas' cultural identity is proof of the power of language to forge connections and barriers between kin and against others. The telling of the story expressed to their clansman Edward Dozier the Arizona Tewas' pride in being Tewa. He was a witness to their cultural survival.

Years later, the anthropologist Fred Eggan, who had conducted fieldwork at Hopi during the 1930s and who became a mentor to Dozier, reflected on Dozier's special relationship with the Hopi-Tewas: "Out there, too, they were more open.... they had secrets and so on which they kept from the Hopi, but they didn't keep them from him. You see, what he did when he went there, he told me some time ago, was to just concentrate on the Hopi-Tewa.... And since he could speak the language, he could get started right away. The people considered him a relative to live with, an ideal situation [in which] to study" (Fred Eggan, interview, May 12, 1988).

Despite the cooperation of his Hopi-Tewa relatives, Dozier soon discovered a problem with his dissertation proposal for a Tewa language study. The predicament arose from his initial premise that the people of Tewa Village, unlike their Rio Grande kin, spoke and preserved a relatively pure ancestral Tewa. To the contrary, his early fieldwork revealed that the Arizona Tewas considered the Rio Grande Pueblos, not themselves, to be the true speakers of the language. Dozier assessed that the Hopi-Tewa dialect had indeed diverged substantially from the ancestral form. Consequently, he decided that a historical linguistic study was inappropriate for Tewa Village and revised his topic. His new dissertation proposal was to study intertribal culture change at Tewa Village, describing the dynamics of 250 years of cultural interaction between the Tewas and Hopis at First Mesa (Emory Sekaquaptewa, interview, April 20, 1994).

Still, he did not discard the topic of language altogether. In the published version of his dissertation he correlated the Hopi-Tewas' language competencies—in Tewa, Hopi, English, and Navajo—with their status as tribal interpreters and facilitators of the 1936 Hopi constitution (Dozier 1954a:302). He also produced an orthography and compared and contrasted Arizona Tewa with Rio Grande Tewa (1954a:261–62). In his dissertation and a later paper Dozier compared Arizona Tewa kinship terms with those of the Santa Clara Tewas, interpreting the former's usage as a reflection of the matrilineal pattern of the Hopis rather than the bilateral descent system of the Rio Grande Pueblos (Dozier 1954a:305–11, 1955a).

Although the Arizona Tewas extended generosity and hospitality to their Rio Grande "kinsman," precisely how they were related historically was unclear. In the 1940s and 1950s, anthropologists identified the Arizona Tewas at Hano as Tano (Thano), or southern Tewa (Reed 1943, 1952). Some scholars questioned whether a real or even a perceived relationship existed between the

Arizona group and the Rio Grande, or northern, Tewas (Dozier 1954a:263–68, 1951). The Tanos had a complex history of migrations northward during the seventeenth century, from the Galisteo Basin southeast of Santa Fe, New Mexico, to the Santa Cruz Valley near Española and Santa Clara Pueblo, and then to the Hopi mesas in 1696. On the basis of ethnohistorical research, Dozier speculated that movements and resettlements of people after the Pueblo Revolt of 1680 had been common. It was possible that some Rio Grande Tewas had joined the Tano community and moved to Hopi (Dozier 1954a:263, n. 2).

More than two centuries later, the descendants of the people who had moved to First Mesa were split over the issue of cultural affiliation. Members of the older generation called themselves Thano Tewas, whereas the younger people called themselves Tewas. In 1936 the progressive activists at Hano had officially changed their town's name, under the Hopi constitution, to Tewa Village (Dozier 1952:1; Hopi Tribe 1936:Article III, Sec. 1). When Dozier came to Tewa Village in 1949, he entered into an "essentially contested" (Gallie 1968) historical discourse in which the Arizona Tewas' identity as Tewas was created and re-created through clan migration stories.

Dozier recognized such political factionalism from personal experience. With his dual identity as both a Pueblo Indian and an anthropologist, "which one of these factions a stranger identified himself [with] was extreamly important" to his field relationships at Tewa Village (EPD4.2, Running Narrative, summer 1949:7). Factionalism at Santa Clara fell along moiety lines (Dozier 1966c), but at Tewa Village it manifested itself along clan lines. Dozier quickly recognized that social organization at Tewa Village (and in the other western pueblos) was very different from that among the Rio Grande villages. In an undated manuscript he summed up the situation for the eastern pueblos:

Among the Tanoans [Tiwas, Tewas, and Towas], with the Towa pueblo of Jemez excepted, there are no clans. The Tewa have clan names: which former investigators have thought to be kinship units like those of Keresan and Hopi clans (Hodge 1896; Harrington 1907–8). Actually, however, these "clan names" do not designate social units of any kind, but are ceremonial terms thought variously to be inherited from one's father or mother. These terms also appear useful in establishing friendly relations in occasional visits to Keresan, Zuni and Hopi villages, but otherwise they have no structural or functional representation among the Tewa. (EPD4.4, "Social Structure of the Rio Grande Tewa Pueblos," n.d.:4)

At Tewa Village, in contrast—as among the Hopis—clans were the central social organizing principle. Years earlier, in an 1894 article titled "The Kinship of a Tanoan Speaking Community in Tusayan," the anthropologist Jesse Walter Fewkes had explained that cultural identity for the Arizona Tewas was based on membership in a matrilineal clan. A person was regarded as Tewa if his or her mother was Tewa, if the person belonged to one of the Tewa clans, and if the person spoke the Tewa language (Fewkes 1894:165–67). Clan affiliation dictated to whom someone was related, whom one could marry, from whom one could expect assistance, whom one was obliged to help, and with what kinship terms one should address others. In general, matrilineal clans organized all social interactions on the Hopi mesas.

In looking at matters of descent, especially that of children born of marriages between Arizona Tewas and Hopis, Dozier agreed with Fewkes: "As long as the mother has a trace of Tewa the children are considered Tewa (the term Tewa is largely a cultural term since in reality very little Tewa blood is actually present). To be Tewa, at least on First Mesa, seems to be a mark of distinction" (EPD 4.2, field notes on Hopi-Tewa ceremonial system, n.d.).

Dozier regarded clan migration stories as historical narratives that claimed and rationalized the Arizona Tewas' social status, prestige, and land rights on First Mesa. In his field diary he wrote:

> In attempting to get at this basic core I have decided to get the migration myths of all the clans involved at Tewa

> village. Each varies to some extent I have been told. But the basic pattern seems to be the same with the rest of the Hopi—who came first to Hopi, seems to be the important thing. At the moment two clans—the Stick and the Bear are rivals. . . . each claims that they came first. (EPD4.2, field diary, December 6, 1949)

In a letter to his fiancée, Marianne Fink, in June 1950 he described the Arizona Tewas' migration from the Santa Cruz Valley, New Mexico, to Hopi country in the late seventeenth century in terms of clan histories:

> The Tewa came to First Mesa upon the invitation of [the Hopi] Bear Clan and Snake Clan—both had been here for a long time and they made agreements as to land, etc. Now both Bear and Snake clans are extinct on First Mesa, but the Tewa will not relinquish the land and rights [they] obtained from Bear Clan and Snake Clan—First Mesa is aware of this also, although the clans are extinct. Hence they will not take land away from the Tewa. (EPD4.1, Dozier to Fink, June 12, 1950)

Although clan membership was the central organizing principle at Tewa Village, the clans were associated with moieties that controlled the two village kivas. The Central Kiva (MunE Te) was identified with the Summer moiety and was the kiva of the village chief. The Outside Kiva (Pende te) was identified with the Winter moiety. The clans associated with the Central Kiva were the Sun (extinct), Tobacco, Corn, and Bear clans, and those associated with the Outside Kiva were the Earth, Cloud, and Cottonwood clans (Dozier 1954a:344). In his notes, under the heading "The Winter Solstice," Dozier wrote that his "allegiance [was] strictly with the Central Kiva," which "determined Tewa thinking to a large extent" (EPD4.2, field notes, December 1949:2). This situation reflected an interesting reversal of moiety affiliation for Dozier, who belonged to the Winter side at Santa Clara Pueblo through his mother's father, José Domingo Gutierrez.

Edward Dozier's dual identities, academic and Indian, converged as he conducted fieldwork at Tewa Village. On First Mesa he acquired ethnographic knowledge that he fused with his cultural knowledge from Santa Clara Pueblo. Conducting field research with his clan relatives both fulfilled his scholarly obligation as a professional anthropologist and found acceptability within the Tewas' cultural framework of reciprocal obligations. His field experiences created for him a special professional and personal identity that blended two contradictory identities into that of an American Indian scholar.

Dozier defended his dissertation, "The Changing Social Organization of the Hopi-Tewa," on December 20, 1951. His core committee consisted of Walter Goldschmidt (chairman), Harry Hoijer, and Ralph Beals. After passing his exams and completing his dissertation, Dozier was officially awarded a Ph.D. in 1952 and so became the first graduate of UCLA's new doctoral program in anthropology.

His colleagues, reviewing his dissertation upon its publication in the University of California series *Publications in American Archaeology and Ethnology* (Dozier 1954a), recognized the synchronicity of scholarship and kinship that Dozier had experienced at Tewa Village (Eggan 1955; Fathauer 1955; Ortiz 1966). One writer, the archaeologist Watson Smith, commended Dozier on his clarity and "objective presentation":

> Certainly no one could be better qualified for this task than the author, who is a Tewa of Santa Clara Pueblo, as well as a trained ethnologist. Being both bilingual and bicultural he has been able to meet the Hopi-Tewa almost as a kinsman and to interpret their culture lucidly in Anglo-American terms....
>
> This paper is, in sum, not only an excellent ethnographic report on a single small village, with important archaeological implications.... Not the least of its virtues lies in the simplicity and lucidity of Dozier's English. He is capable of expressing himself adequately without resort to

the esoteric jargon which beclouds some anthropological writing. One may infer that his facility with his native Tewa is equally fluent, a fact that adds measureably [*sic*] to the reader's confidence in his understanding and interpretation of his informants. (Smith 1956:325)

The anthropologist Robert H. Lowie was equally supportive of Dozier's academic credentials and dissertation in his review, published in the German journal *Sociologus:*

> The present publication is . . . unique, as the author has, as ethnologist, taken a degree at a respectable university but at the same time is a Tewa Indian born in Santa Clara, New Mexico, who can communicate with ease in Hano, Arizona, with the Hopi Tewa . . . and who is received by them as a welcome guest. In order to respect this last mentioned fact one must have tried to do fieldwork with a Pueblo tribe, as the author of this review has done.
>
> Of greatest importance to the sociologists is Dozier's description of the acculturation processes. . . . his publication is an extremely praiseworthy enrichment of our ethnological literature. (Lowie n.d., translated from the German)

Some years later, when his dissertation was published as a stand-alone ethnography (Dozier 1966a), the editors of the series, "Case Studies in Cultural Anthropology," emphasized to their student audience the uniqueness of the work and its author:

> This case study is unusual. It was written by a man who knows Hano, the Tewa Indian community of which he writes, in a somewhat different way than most anthropologists know pueblo communities. He is accepted as a friend, as an insider, and speaks the language fluently. He never violates this friendship and acceptance in what he writes about the Tewa, and yet the reader achieves a feeling of directness and intimacy that is often lacking in descriptions of pueblo life. (Spindler and Spindler 1966:v–vi)

Dozier's fieldwork at Tewa Village wove different value systems —those of academic anthropologists, the Arizona Tewas, the Hopis, and the Rio Grande Tewas—into a composite whole, retaining the integrity of both the scholarly discipline and indigenous practices. Dozier negotiated cultural differences and similarities to the mutual benefit of scholarship, the communities involved (he helped strengthen social and ceremonial ties by bringing elders back and forth between the Arizona and New Mexico pueblos), and himself. Unlike the social and political environment of World War II, which had "Americanized" Sergeant Dozier, fieldwork at Tewa Village intensified his relationship with Pueblo Indian culture as well as with academe. His kinship ties with the subjects of his fieldwork at Tewa Village enriched his ethnography and added a new cultural dimension to academic research conducted by an American Indian anthropologist.

In 1952 Dozier graduated from a program that the anthropology department at UCLA described as preparing students "to teach on the college or university level and to engage in original research" (EPD2.4, UCLA, Department of Anthropology, n.d.). For the first time in the history of the discipline, a professionally trained American Indian anthropologist was about to defy the paradox and launch an academic career studying his own indigenous culture, that of the Pueblo Indian communities.

5

"An Indian and a Scholar" in the Academy

> [Dozier was] for his time a great scholar. . . . No one thought of him as an Indian anthropologist, just as an anthropologist who was an Indian.
> —Fred Eggan, interview, May 12, 1988

With a UCLA doctorate in hand, Edward P. Dozier became only the second American Indian to receive a Ph.D. in anthropology—the first had been William Jones, a Sac and Fox, who had earned his degree at Columbia University in 1904. To celebrate Dozier's accomplishment, *Newsweek* published an article in its science section on March 24, 1952, titled "Dozier Dossier." The illustrated piece included a photograph of the new graduate in an intellectual pose, wearing a coat and tie, holding a pipe, and surrounded by books, including a "native arts" book placed prominently before the camera. The portrait was captioned "Dozier: An Indian and a scholar." A relative of Dozier's commented that the significant word in this caption was the conjunction *and*, because it integrated his cultural and intellectual identities. The article concluded with the note that the American Indian anthropologist, who had studied his "distant relatives," the Arizona Tewas, was now writing a book on the subject.

Despite his moment of fame in a national magazine, Dozier still faced the challenge of finding a university position. In the 1940s the profession had been small, numbering about four hundred anthropologists who were all relatively familiar with each other (Rogge 1976). By the 1950s the postwar supply of new Ph.D.s who had funded their higher education on the GI Bill was

Figure 7. Edward P. Dozier, 1952. This portrait appeared in *Newsweek* in March in a short article titled "Dozier Dossier," written in anticipation of Dozier's June doctorate in anthropology from UCLA. The caption read "Dozier: An Indian and a scholar." (Reproduced with permission of Newsweek, Inc.)

growing exponentially. The demand for academic jobs was high, and available teaching positions in anthropology were scarce.

After finishing his fieldwork in Arizona, Dozier was fortunate to be offered a one-year position at the University of Oregon for 1951–52, replacing a faculty member who was on sabbatical leave. There he acquired more teaching experience and wrote his dissertation. In April 1952 he returned to Tewa Village with six students from the University of Oregon to conduct ethnological research for eight weeks (Spicer Papers, Dozier to E. Spicer, April 30, 1952). For the 1952–53 academic year he received a postdoctoral fellowship from the Wenner-Gren Foundation for Anthropological Research to write a monograph on the Hopi-Tewas for the University of California's series in archaeology and ethnology (Dozier 1954a).

With a referral from Edward H. Spicer, an eminent Southwestern ethnologist at the University of Arizona, and with his status as a John Hay Whitney Opportunity Fellow, Dozier was chosen for a lucrative job in the summer of 1953 sponsored by the Ford Foundation's Fund for the Advancement of Education. He and his wife, Marianne, who had an MA in psychology from the University of New Mexico, worked on a study of segregation and integration in Arizona and New Mexico public schools. The Ford Foundation study provided them not only with scholarly work but also ample money to pay off their college debts and purchase land in Corrales, New Mexico, for a summer house (Dozier family interview, July 12, 1990).

Like any other job seeker, Dozier drew on his network of family friends, former professors, colleagues, and mentors as he searched for a faculty appointment. This network sustained him throughout his twenty-year career in anthropology. Dozier was fortunate to have inherited his father's connections with early Southwestern anthropologists, including Barbara Freire-Marreco (Aitken) in England, John P. Harrington at the Bureau of American Ethnology, and Oliver La Farge at the Association on American Indian Affairs. Over the years, he added to this network his own mentors, colleagues in Southwestern anthropology, and lifetime friends, among them W.W. Hill, Florence Hawley Ellis, and Leslie Spier at UNM, Harry Hoijer at UCLA, Edward Spicer at the University of Arizona, Carl Voegelin at Indiana University, Fred Eggan at the University of Chicago, and Elizabeth Shepley Sergeant, by now living in Rockland County, New York. Within the academy and in dealings with external associations and foundations, they advocated for him and promoted him as a colleague.

An early example is the way the university network assisted Dozier in the search for his first faculty position. Fred Eggan recalled that a year after Dozier defended his dissertation, "Harry Hoijer [at UCLA]) recommended him to [Melville] Herskovits," a UCLA-trained ethnologist and linguist at Northwestern University in Illinois (Fred Eggan, interview, May 12, 1988). With his credentials and the support of his network, Dozier was offered his first job at Northwestern University.

In 1953 Marianne Dozier described Edward's job offer from Northwestern in a letter to Edward Spicer's wife, Rosamond: "[William] Bascom wrote asking Ed if he wanted a year's job as instructor, teaching 8 hours. He accepted—so it's to Evanston we'll go this fall (brrr. . . .)" (Spicer Papers, M. Dozier to R. Spicer, June 13, 1953). The couple would have to adapt to "Chicago's miserable climate" (Spicer Papers, E. Dozier to E. Spicer, January 4, 1957), and Dozier would have to adjust to Northwestern's intellectual orientation. Its anthropology department was renowned for its African Studies program, under the direction of Melville Herskovits. Dozier, as a Southwestern anthropologist, "didn't have much in common with Herskovits" (Fred Eggan, interview, May 12, 1988). He aptly described his position at Northwestern as that of "an Americanist among Africanists" (EPD4.1, Dozier to Spier, April 27, 1957).

With the sensitive eyes of a new hire, instructor Dozier observed that most doctoral students in cultural anthropology at Northwestern received "a liberal grant for research in Africa," particularly in "folklore [and] acculturation studies" (EPD4.1, Dozier to Gerry [no surname], November 4, 1954). He elaborated on the scope of the faculty's research:

> Let me characterize Northwestern's anthropology department. Northwestern, as you undoubtedly know, stresses Africa—both in course work and in research. Herskovits and Bascom have had extensive field experience in Africa

and teach with considerable competence gained from first hand knowledge, various aspects of African culture: Religion, Political Institutions, Art, etc. [Richard] Waterman is primarily a musicologist but has field experience in the West Indies and Australia and teaches courses on Oceanea and Australia. Francis Hsu is Chinese as you may know. He has published extensively on culture and personality and also on American and Chinese national character. He offers courses on social organization, the far east and on culture and personality. I teach linguistics and courses on the American Indian. (EPD4.1, Dozier to Gerry [no surname], November 4, 1954)

Acting chair William Bascom assigned Dozier to teach a night course on the American Indian at Northwestern's downtown campus on the semester system. Later he taught courses in language and linguistics at the Evanston campus on the quarter system. Although he enjoyed teaching at Northwestern, his cultural and academic identity remained solidly in the Southwest (Spicer Papers, M. Dozier to R. Spicer, April 24, 1955).

It was at Northwestern University, as a tenure-track faculty member in the 1950s, that Edward Dozier became the first American Indian academic anthropologist. He quickly advanced from instructor (1953–54) to assistant professor (1954–57) and then associate professor (1958–59). Besides teaching and fulfilling the university's service requirement for promotion and tenure, he conformed to the academy's "publish or perish" dictate by writing a steady stream of papers and book reviews for publication. During his employment at Northwestern he produced twenty-two publications—one monograph, thirteen articles, seven book reviews, and one review of conference papers. He wrote in a style that was generally free of scholarly jargon, so his publications were accessible and understandable to a broad audience. During these years his writings often consisted of works taking descriptive and historical approaches to linguistic and acculturation studies of Pueblo Indians.

Dozier wrote his 1954 monograph on the Arizona Tewas, too, in the genre of an acculturation study—a genre that partially constrained his interpretations (Kroskrity 1993). Drawing on historical, linguistic, economic, political, ceremonial, and kinship data, he described the dynamics of cultural change in an American Indian society that had experienced prolonged contact with a neighboring, dominant Pueblo community, the Hopis. With the 1954 work Dozier began slowly to infuse American Indian values into the anthropological literature. In it he contributed subtle innovations to the standard formula of the acculturation text, in which Indians acquiesced to the dominant white culture.

Dozier interpreted culture change as a complex historical process that involved cultural and psychological adaptations. The process was simultaneously integrative (people incorporated select borrowed traits) and resistant (they retained specific native customs). Instead of focusing his research on Indian-white relations, the usual subject of acculturation studies, he chose to study the dynamics of relations between the Arizona Tewas and the Hopis on First Mesa. Through language, the two groups adapted to their consolidated mesa community, and the Hopi-Tewas preserved core elements of their cultural identity as Tewas (Dozier 1954a:290–97). For example, Dozier showed how the Arizona Tewas served as interpreters and cultural brokers to facilitate intercultural exchanges at Hopi and were simultaneously keepers of a "language curse" that denied the Hopis access to their ancestral language.

With these insights Dozier offered a new, indigenous perspective on the anthropological theory of acculturation. In his research at Tewa Village he identified and explored intertribal relationships and culture change. With his understanding of Indian-to-Indian acculturation processes, shaped by the kinship and language he shared with the Arizona Tewas, Dozier contributed a native voice to academic anthropology. Unfortunately, with the notable exceptions of Watson Smith's and Robert Lowie's reviews of Dozier's monograph (Lowie n.d.; Smith 1956), his innovation in "indigenous-based theory" (Jones 1970) went generally unrecognized at the time.

Dozier also analyzed the selectivity of borrowing in several other comparative studies he made of culture contact—Spanish and Indian (Dozier 1954b), Yaqui and Tewa (Dozier 1956a), Spanish Catholic and Rio Grande Pueblo (Dozier 1958b). To him acculturation was both a theory and a practice. Just as he himself had deliberately chosen to assimilate into the white academic world, so the extent of change on the part of other individuals or societies was, in full or in part, a matter of choice.

One aspect of acculturation theory in the 1950s did constrain Dozier's interpretation of social change at Tewa Village. It was the concept of "compartmentalization," an intellectual construct often employed by American ethnographers from the mid-1930s to the early 1960s. Within the overall framework of acculturation theory, compartmentalization referred to one phase of adjustment made by American Indians—that in which they accepted certain traits from the dominant white society but kept them separate or isolated from their indigenous customs. Compartmentalization was considered a transitional phase of culture contact; it was "an adaptive process, reducing conflicts between new and old traits by keeping them separate and gaining time for internal adjustments, reinterpretation, and selective incorporation into the host culture" (Singer 1976:231). In his own research Dozier identified seven other types of acculturative adjustments: rejection, assimilation, fusion, incorporation, reactive adaptation, stabilized pluralism, and off-reservation and urban adjustments (EPD4.4, "Reaction of American Indians to Euro-American Contact," ca. 1968).

Dozier was introduced to compartmentalization through the work of Edward Spicer. After reading Spicer's publications, particularly his 1954 article "Spanish-Indian Acculturation in the Southwest," and after participating with Spicer in the Inter-University Summer Research Seminar in Albuquerque in 1956, Dozier developed a strong interest in and commitment to this theoretical construct. The seminar, a cross-cultural study of bilingualism sponsored by the Social Science Research Council, brought Dozier into contact with some major Southwestern ethnologists—Edward M. Bruner, Helene Codere, David H. French, and Evon Z. Vogt, in addition to Spicer. The project resulted in an important edited volume on acculturation, *Perspectives in American Indian Culture Change* (Spicer 1961), to which Dozier contributed an article on Pueblo Indian culture contact that developed his ideas on compartmentalization.

Dozier recognized that the Rio Grande Pueblos, responding to colonialism strategically, had survived with their cultures modified but essentially intact. This theme in Dozier's writing (e.g., 1961a) complemented Spicer's concept of the "persistence of ethnic enclaves" (Spicer 1962). At Northwestern University Dozier experimented with compartmentalization as a means to explain the "coexistence" of the indigenous and Spanish Catholic religions in Rio Grande Pueblo communities. He developed a theory of culture change that described how the Pueblos had constructed cultural boundaries to lessen the threat of Christianity to Pueblo spirituality.

In 1955 he presented his ideas on compartmentalization at the annual meeting of the American Anthropological Association in Boston. His paper, "The Values and Moral Concepts of the Rio Grande Pueblo Indians," revealed his formative thoughts:

> Although the Spaniards exerted strong pressures and effected important changes, the core of Rio Grande Pueblo culture seems not to have been drastically altered. Rather, the Rio Grande Pueblos adopted Spanish culture and religion as an added system distinct from their own. The indigenous system of values and moral concepts gave coherence and integration to both systems. It is important to discuss this phenomenon in some detail for it appears to be a unique type of acculturation and throws light on differences in value systems and concepts of the two groups. (EPD4.4; also see Dozier 1956c)

Dozier's acculturation studies were accepted into the mainstream of anthropological literature. Leading anthropologists such as Edward Spicer praised his ethnographic and ethnohistorical work. Spicer wrote to Dozier about a chapter he had written on the Rio Grande Pueblos (Dozier 1961a) for a book Spicer was editing: "I don't know of any account of acculturation which gives so effectively the picture of the changing conditions to which a native group has been required to adapt. Somehow you manage to describe or suggest what seem to me the really significant conditions with a vividness that is hard to match in the literature" (EPD4.1, Spicer to Dozier, February 14, 1958).

Dozier applied the concept of compartmentalization to Pueblo religion and illustrated how selective adaptations to directed culture change were intended to preserve the traditional core of ceremonial life. Although he acknowledged the existence of compartmentalization among the Pueblos by the late eighteenth century, his emphasis was not on the purity of the separateness (for example, the absence of Spanish Catholic elements in indigenous religious practices) but rather on the community's "intentions" or desire to keep the traditions distinct (Dozier 1961a:176). In the eyes of some contemporaneous scholars, such as Florence Hawley Ellis, compartmentalization led to the complete amalgamation of native and Spanish traits over time. To Pueblo people and those anthropologists with native sensibilities, such as Dozier, it was a deliberate strategy of cultural preservation. This focus on the persistence of Pueblo culture rather than on assimilation made Dozier's ethnographic analysis subtly and significantly distinct and infused a native perspective into the anthropological theory of acculturation.

One reform Dozier proposed was that anthropologists rethink the terms they employed to represent indigenous people. In his article "The Concepts of 'Primitive' and 'Native'" (1955c) he argued for modernizing postcolonial representations of the other, who was now literate and more informed in the postwar era and in emerging third-world nations. He encouraged respect for the modern cultures and persons described in the anthropological literature, and he advocated the selection of terms that were mutually acceptable to social scientists and local communities. Positioning himself as an intermediary, he wrote about anthropologists' "dual responsibilities" to the discipline and to postcolonial societies:

> Anthropologists are... in the precarious position of having to select terms which are adequate taxonomic and descriptive designations as well as terms which do not evoke a clamor of negative reaction from the public-at-large. This is felt more keenly today because the societies which anthropologists traditionally have studied are themselves in a ferment of change. The impact of industrialized civilization is penetrating into the most marginal and isolated areas of the world. In the process, large numbers of "nonliterates" are becoming literate and participants in "non-primitive" cultures. Anthropologists, therefore, have the task of selecting designations which satisfy the requirement of their science and which do not offend the sensibilities of large numbers of people. (Dozier 1955c:187–88)

Dozier acknowledged colonialism and recommended changes in the scientific language to better reflect the contemporary conditions of indigenous people. He showed that the term *primitive*, derived from nineteenth-century social evolutionism, implied racial inferiority in colonially subjugated people. He exposed the emergent consciousness of newly literate people and expressed their disapproval of the "negatively charged terminology by which they often are characterized" in anthropological texts (Dozier 1955c:198). Although he suggested that less value-laden terms such as *nonliterate* might be more acceptable, he admitted in this case that the word might be confused with the derogatory *illiterate* (Dozier 1955c:196–97). He cautioned that

> we must realize that this literature reaches not only large numbers of literate peoples of industrialized societies, but also members of societies which have been the subject of

anthropological study. Indeed, many of these people are themselves in professional positions, such as teachers, lawyers, medical doctors—even anthropologists. . . . They are strongly affected by the work of anthropologists, especially with the literature devoted to them and most particularly with the terminology used. (Dozier 1955c:195)

In this passage Dozier identified himself as one of those literate professionals—an anthropologist—who was also a tribal member. Like his fellow postcolonial others, he was "strongly affected" by anthropological terms used to describe American Indians. Speaking with the dual authority of his Pueblo and professional identities, he proposed changes in the vocabulary of the discipline that would improve relationships between anthropologists and members of non-Western communities. He consciously worked to renegotiate the scientific relationship between subject and object and called for a professional ethics and public accountability. For Dozier, with ties to both Anglo and Indian communities, anthropology had broader implications for cultural inclusivity. His discourse crossed borders of self and other and bridged the emic and etic perspectives of anthropology. His experience with otherness was for Dozier an encounter with self, and his professional practice integrated scientific objectivity and indigenous worldviews in the pursuit of knowledge.

Fewer than ten years after Dozier published his article advocating a more culturally sensitive terminology to describe native people, a former colleague of his at Northwestern University, Francis L.K. Hsu, a Chinese American, undertook a study of the use of the word *primitive* in the anthropological literature (Hsu 1964). Although the two men's methods were different, their purposes as minority anthropologists were the same. Yet nowhere in Hsu's article did he cite Dozier's earlier work on the topic—a seemingly inexplicable omission, particularly by one of the few contemporary minority practitioners in anthropology.

Hsu's omission raises the question of what effect, if any, Dozier's article had on the profession. Because it was an article and not a book, no reviews of his ideas were written. But if we look at the historical context of his writing, some things are evident. First, the article was published in the prestigious Wenner-Gren Foundation's *Yearbook of Anthropology* for 1955, and Dozier received a prominent position as lead author in the section on theory. Second, he was in the company of such leading anthropologists as Raymond Firth, A.L. Kroeber, Oscar Lewis, David G. Mandelbaum, and Sol Tax, who also contributed to the volume. And third, in the introduction Dozier was given a prominence that was unusual for a new scholar. It said:

> Dozier is symbolic of a coming-of-age by anthropology, not only in the United States but elsewhere. Professional training (Ph.D.) and academic employment (Instructor) has been afforded a scholar of Hopi-Tewa ancestry, who now expresses his views on the anthropological concepts of "primitive" and "native." The historical development of the study of nonliterate societies is reviewed, and a brief account included on field techniques and methods, since the approach to field work is to a large extent influenced by the view of nonliterate societies. Then considered is the impact of the study of anthropology on the lay public and on the members of societies which have been the subject of anthropological study. The problem of selecting terminology for purposes of description and classification is both ethnical and practical. (*Yearbook of Anthropology* 1955:185).

Whether or not Dozier's call for changes in the language of anthropology resonated with practitioners at the time, he clearly was gaining visibility and stature within the profession.

During the mid-1950s, as he wrote his monograph and articles and taught classes about the Pueblo world, Dozier retained his ties to the Southwest more directly by spending summers at the adobe house he and his Santa Clara relatives built in Corrales, New Mexico. His and Marianne's son, Migué, was born in New Mexico in the summer of 1955 while Dozier served as a staff member for the

University of New Mexico's Southwestern Project in Comparative Psycholinguistics.

In 1958–59, an academic year spent as a fellow at Stanford University's Center for Advanced Studies in the Behavioral Sciences raised Dozier's status as a scholar. It also expanded his professional network and opportunities and enabled him to produce a core of Pueblo research from which he derived many future publications. The Doziers' daughter, Anya, was born that March in Palo Alto. The following month Dozier returned to Tewa Village to conduct ethnological research with members of the center's kinship research team—Meyer Fortes, Cornelius Osgood, and I. Waterhouse.

Dozier's increased scholarly recognition brought him prestigious appointments outside of academe. In 1955 he became the first American Indian elected to the board of directors of the Association on American Indian Affairs (AAIA), a national watchdog group for American Indian rights based in New York City (AAIA Archives, Princeton University Library, Seeley G. Mudd Manuscript Library). The organization's goals were "protecting Indians in the enjoyment of their constitutional rights, thwarting federal efforts at forced termination of tribal status, dealing with the effects of urbanization on native peoples, and educating the public at large to their condition" (La Potin 1987:19).

Dozier's connection with this high-profile Indian advocacy group, led by Oliver La Farge, involved him in a hearing by the Senate Subcommittee on Indian Affairs in 1957. At the hearing he read a prepared statement from the AAIA in support of "a bill which will stop termination proceedings" (EPD3.1, Dozier to Sergeant, July 8, 1957). Termination was a federal policy intended to end federal trust responsibilities toward tribes (Deloria and Lytle 1984). During the 1950s, special federal programs were suspended and tribal land sold for more than one hundred terminated tribes (Getches, Wilkinson, and Williams 1993). Pueblo Indian governments and others with concerns about federal trust responsibilities, tribal sovereignty, and the protection of aboriginal land firmly opposed this policy.

As the hearing unfolded, it began to focus not only on the AAIA's policy position but also on Dozier's personal and cultural identity. After Dozier read his statement to the subcommittee, the senators questioned him. When he identified himself as a professor of anthropology at Northwestern University, they respectfully addressed him as "Doctor" and pursued their inquiry into federal trust responsibilities. In a conversation with Senator Barry Goldwater (R-Arizona) on the issue of federal control over the leasing of reservation land, Dozier agreed conditionally: "Yes, Senator. The only thing I would insist upon is that it is done through the consent of the tribe" (U.S. Congress 1958:77). In general, his responses emphasized tribal decision making and a tribe's legal right to seek advice outside the Bureau of Indian Affairs for economic development projects.

The tone of the hearings changed when Senator George W. Malone (R-Nevada), an advocate of terminating the federal trust relationship with tribes—including economic and social services provided to them—harshly criticized reservations. To Malone, American Indian reservations were "concentration camps." Dozier asked him to "revise" the statement, but the senator rebutted, asking Dozier whether he had ever lived on a reservation. It was only then that Dozier identified himself as an American Indian at the hearing. Malone then took the offensive, hammering Dozier with questions about his experiences as an Indian:

> **Malone:** Did you ever live on one [a reservation]?
> **Dozier:** Yes; I happen to be an American Indian myself.
> **Malone:** Which one was it?
> **Dozier:** Again, Senator, I must say that I do not consider it a concentration camp.
> **Malone:** Tell me where you lived?
> **Dozier:** I lived in a community and I love my community.
> **Malone:** Where?
> **Dozier:** In New Mexico.
> **Malone:** Is it a reservation?
> **Dozier:** Yes.

Malone: Which one?
Dozier: Santa Clara Pueblo.
Malone: What is its status?
Dozier: It is still a pueblo.
Malone: What are the arrangements surrounding it? What are the rules and regulations surrounding an Indian there that is on the reservation?
Dozier: Well, Senator, in order to explain that I am afraid I will keep the committee here for a long time.
Malone: I think you could probably explain it if you wanted to.
Dozier: Let me say there are, as far as I can see, no restrictions on my person.
Malone: I am not talking about you. I am talking about the people who are there.
Dozier: I am using myself as an example of an individual from my own tribe. Let me say that one can leave or come from the pueblo at will. I have been away many years. I have also lived in the pueblo off and on. I did not leave my village until I was about 10 years old. I spent almost the entire period of my first 10 years in the pueblo.
Malone: How did you come to leave?
Dozier: I wanted to get schooling. My parents placed me in an Indian school in Santa Fe, N. Mex., which was the pattern in those days. You went out of your village into a boarding school. I received my education there. I then went to the University of New Mexico and received a bachelor of arts degree, master of arts degree, then on to the University of California at Los Angeles, where I received my doctor of philosophy degree. (U.S. Congress 1958:81–82)

A lengthy discussion ensued about Dozier's personal experiences and about available funding for Indian education. Malone, who favored private ownership of land, emphasized that Indian students could not claim individual economic rights to reservation land owned in common by the tribe. To him reservations represented socialism and obstacles to assimilation. Dozier, as an American Indian anthropologist and spokesperson for the AAIA, strongly disagreed. His advocacy for American Indian rights has now become part of the congressional record.

The late 1950s were years of challenge and change in Edward Dozier's career. He was lonely at Northwestern University, the sole Southwesternist among Africanists. As a consequence, he developed stronger personal and professional bonds with Fred Eggan and his wife, Dorothy, at the University of Chicago. Their ethnographic knowledge of the Hopis was a comfort to Edward and Marianne. The Doziers also learned of the new Philippine Studies program that Eggan had started at Chicago, under the sponsorship of the Carnegie Corporation (Eggan 1954).

Like Dozier, Eggan was a World War II veteran of the Pacific theater and had become interested in Philippine cultures. When they both spent a year at the Center for Advanced Study at Stanford in 1958–59, Eggan planted the idea that Dozier should study a culture radically different from that of the Pueblo Southwest. He suggested that Dozier plan an ethnographic study of the Kalinga people of northern Luzon in the Philippines. Eggan believed such a study would aid in Dozier's professional development, expand his knowledge of world cultures, and add a comparative perspective to his scholarship. He later recalled:

> The reason that I was interested in sending Ed there was for his own education. Growing up in the Pueblo . . . [with] the need for secrecy and so forth, I thought it would be good for Ed to . . . see a society like [those of] the [Philippine] mountain valleys. They are anxious to help you. You ask them a question, they say, "Well, nobody here knows anything about that, but there's someone on the other side of the mountain." And they'll run over there and bring the guy back . . . and it's done for you. You want to know that you can ask a question, and you can get an answer. Well, that's the kind of situation that sometimes Chuck [Lange]

and I wish happened along the Rio Grande here. (Fred Eggan, interview, May 12, 1988)

Dozier took his mentor's advice. In a letter to the Social Science Research Council, he explained his research interest in the Philippines:

> The proposed project has no relation to my Ph.D. thesis; it is in a new area and on a different problem. Work that I have more recently done in the American Southwest has relevance to the proposed study, however. Among the Pueblos of New Mexico, for example, I have investigated the transition of these societies from lineage-based groups to the development of centralized villages. The Kalinga in the Mountain Provinces present the next step beyond; that is, organization into a federation of villages. It is this shift and the mechanisms by which it is accomplished that interests me. (EPD4.5, Dozier to Social Science Research Council, ca. 1958)

Later he successfully applied to the National Science Foundation for a senior postdoctoral grant to fund his fieldwork in the Philippines.

Dozier gave ample credit to Fred and Dorothy Eggan in the prefaces to his two Kalinga ethnographies. In the first, published in 1966, he wrote: "My debt to Professor and Mrs. Fred Eggan is immeasurable. They first aroused my interest in the peoples of the Mountain Province and assisted in many ways in making our field work in the Philippines a pleasant experience. Professor Eggan followed my work in the field and has read this study critically in final draft" (Dozier 1966b:x).

In July 1959 Dozier and his family flew to Manila and then set up a home in Baguio City, to the north. Under an institutional affiliation with the University of the Philippines' Institute of Asian Studies, Dozier began a year of ethnographic study, from August 1959 to August 1960. Even while he was planning a new research project in an unfamiliar East Asian culture area, he was negotiating an offer of a job as a professor of linguistics at the University of Arizona—a chance to return to the Southwest. In the fall of 1959 the Department of Anthropology at Arizona hired him with the rank of full professor; while in the Philippines, he was listed as on leave without pay. The Southwest would have to wait.

During the 1950s Edward Dozier achieved what no other American Indian had at that time—he became a tenured professor of anthropology in the academy. At last he was in a position to influence the discipline and the broader university culture regarding American Indian issues and values. He had established a reputation as a distinguished Pueblo Indian scholar and had opened a path for American Indians who dreamed of an academic career studying their own or other cultures.

6

Fieldwork with the Anthropological Other, the Kalingas

Field work among the Kalinga is in great contrast to investigations among the Pueblos. There is none of the secretiveness and resistance that is general in the Rio Grande Pueblo area.
    —Edward Dozier to Emil Haury, September 15, 1959

An archetype in anthropology is the romantic image of the ethnographer who travels to distant lands to conduct fieldwork amid exotic cultures (Gupta and Ferguson 1997:11; Stocking 1992). But the image also underlies a basic truth about anthropology, namely, that fieldwork is central to understanding the diversity of global cultures. Consequently, the final rite of passage for Edward Dozier in anthropology—the step that would complete his professional credentials in the discipline—was to study a non-Indian culture outside of North America.

The academic rewards for studying the "anthropological other" were very real. According to the norms of the profession at the time, an indigenous anthropologist was at best provincial, because his knowledge was limited to his own cultural community. At worst he was an anomaly, with a lesser, minority status in the academy. By shifting his research to the Philippines, Dozier could avoid the stereotype of the native anthropologist. He could develop a dual expertise as both an "insider" anthropologist—one who studied his own people—and an "outsider" anthropologist—one who studied a foreign culture. Although Dozier was a recognized scholar of the Pueblo Indians, his status would improve because of his fieldwork in the Philippines. As a scholar of the Kalingas he would possess full and all-inclusive rights in academic anthropology.

Although Dozier himself might not have subscribed to the proposition that his Kalinga research authenticated him as an anthropologist, his colleagues recognized the advantages of his conducting fieldwork in the Philippines. Not only would it be a means of crossing a professional barrier that existed for him as an indigenous Southwestern anthropologist, it would also initiate him into "problem-based" anthropological research. Under Fred Eggan's tutelage, Dozier shifted his focus from the direct historical approach of the Boasian tradition to the more controlled comparative method influenced by A.R. Radcliffe-Brown's structuralism, then in vogue at the University of Chicago. Years later, Emil Haury, chair of the Department of Anthropology at the University of Arizona, described the pedagogical value of Dozier's Philippine research:

> We'll go back to [the] philosophical basis of the people that are involved in a department. They can be too narrow, too tunnel-visioned. And if they are, in my opinion, they lose their real impact upon the students.
>
> So that I think that Ed's going to the Philippines . . . was a good move because it gave Ed a comparative base, not only the Tewa that he knew well, but it would give him a comparative base to see how some other people behaved, why, and what. And that would make him a better anthropologist. (Emil Haury, interview, June 5, 1990)

His fieldwork in the mountains of northern Luzon and his related publications brought a new dimension to Dozier's scholarship. During his tenure at the University of Arizona in the 1960s he published his first book on the Kalingas, *Mountain Arbiters: The Changing Life of a Philippine Hill People* (Dozier 1966b), through the university press. Following a pattern he had established with his Arizona Tewa monograph, he also produced a case study, *The Kalinga of Northern Luzon, Philippines* (Dozier 1967a), part of a series in cultural anthropology for undergraduate students published by Holt, Rinehart and Winston. Having fulfilled the traditional role of the social scientist who studies and publishes on an alien culture, Dozier successfully completed his rite of passage for full status in academic anthropology.

To any American anthropologist, native or non-native, the Kalingas and other regional cultures in the mountains of the northern Philippines personified exoticism and otherness. In sharp contrast to the anthropological representation of Pueblo Indian cultures as peaceful and egalitarian (Benedict 1934), the Kalingas had acquired a reputation as a notorious headhunting and cannibal society—the antithesis of civilized society (see White 1978).

William Jones (1871–1909), the first American Indian to earn a Ph.D. in anthropology, had labeled them "the wild men of Luzon" (quoted in Rosaldo 1980:24). In what must be one of the strangest coincidences in anthropological history, Jones, a Boasian-trained Sac and Fox indigenous scholar (Jones 1901, 1904, 1905, 1907) who was working for Chicago's Field Museum of Natural History, had gone to the Philippines early in the twentieth century to conduct fieldwork with the Kalingas' neighbors, the Ilongots. Even more remarkably, the Ilongots validated their and their neighbors' reputation as headhunters by murdering Jones on his last day of fieldwork (Rideout 1912). Years later, Dozier would express his own interpretation of this event.

From an anthropological perspective, the Kalingas were perfect for scholarly study—they were "cut from a traditional ethnographic mold . . . exotic enough to command interest and sufficiently self-contained to justify holistic analysis" (Rosaldo 1980:8). Moreover, they fitted into the prescribed relationship between a scientist and a "primitive" society (see Hinsley 1981). That is, an anthropologist, as a civilized scholar representing a highly developed intellectual tradition, studied the simple society and culture of headhunters.

By the time Dozier went to the Philippines, headhunting was a thing of the past, although the stereotype continued in the popular press. When Dozier returned to the United States, an Arizona newspaper greeted his arrival in Tucson with the headline "New UA Prof is fresh from head-hunting tribe." But in fact colonial authorities had suppressed headhunting in the Philippines in the early twentieth century. By 1959, when Dozier arrived, the Kalingas and surrounding tribes had replaced blood feuds with a "peace pact" system of regional alliances as a way of arbitrating disputes. Dozier himself wrote emphatically about the absence of headhunting among the Kalingas at mid-twentieth century. In a letter to a colleague in Baguio City, where he lived while doing his fieldwork, he later reported:

> In the North Kalinga—*No head hunting ritual is performed today*. . . . All is forgotten now—only partially remembered by the very old. They wouldn't do a head hunting ritual now anyway—because they don't want to offend other Kalingas—not because of fear of the government necessarily.
>
> My information comes from old men in Salegseg and Mabaca.
>
> What little fragments of former head hunting rites exist today—such as boasting about killings by old men at peace pact celebrations and other minor bits—can hardly be equated with the former, elaborate headhunting rite.
>
> I repeat: This is for *North Kalinga*—I am not vouching for Southern Kalinga, Bontocs or Ifugaos—only for the area of my study. (EPD4.1, Dozier to Larry [Wilson], ca. 1960s)

In any case, Dozier never intended simply to write an ethnography of the Kalingas, headhunters or not. Under Eggan's influence, he chose a "problem-focused" approach in order to study the "shift from kinship-based [social] organizations to larger territorially organized groups," as suggested by an earlier ethnographer of Kalinga culture, Roy Franklin Barton (1949). Incorporating Dozier's long-standing interest in social organization, the study was intended to test Barton's "economic-ecological hypothesis," which proposed that "important social and cultural differences" between the northern and southern Kalingas were correlated with differences in the two groups' basic economies (EPD4.3, report on the Penrose Fund grant, ca. 1962).

The northern Kalingas, mostly dry rice cultivators with a kinship-based society, lived in the uplands and were fewer in number than the more densely settled southern Kalingas, who were predominantly wet rice farmers with, apparently, a territorially based society. Barton's basic assumption had been that wet rice cultivation was an effective subsistence strategy that supported large numbers of territorially organized people—an emergent state formation—in the southern Kalinga area (Department of Anthropology, University of Arizona, departmental employee records, Edward Dozier, project report, ca. 1960). Eventually Dozier would discover that Barton had been partially right but that historical factors also played a role in the Kalingas' social organization.

For this project, instead of living full-time in the field as he had done on First Mesa, Dozier accommodated his wife, son, and infant daughter by renting an apartment for the family in Baguio City that "functioned as research headquarters for the year" (Dozier 1966b:xii). From there he anticipated "considerable traveling... in the Mountain Provinces" (EPD4.3, Dozier to SSRC, ca. 1958). As it turned out, he was able to conduct only limited fieldwork in the distant villages because of the considerable effort required to get to them from the city (Dozier 1966b:xii). Travel was difficult, partly because of the risk of mudslides on mountain slopes during the rainy season. In the preface to his 1966 ethnography Dozier described his weekly and monthly field trips from Baguio City to survey the small Kalinga villages: "I lived in Lubuagan with one Kalinga family for one month, and my family joined me later in the hamlet of Alingag (northern Kalinga) for another steady residence of a month. Aside from these periods, I did not maintain prolonged residence in other hamlets. My visits to the regional populations consisted of a week in one hamlet, two weeks in another, and so on" (Dozier 1966b:xiii).

Dozier documented his Kalinga research in five field journals and composition notebooks labeled by region or topic—"Mabaca," "Lubuagan," "Salegseg," "Notes on Lubuagan," and "Songs of Kalinga." In a typical field entry made in August 1959 he recorded

Figure 8. Marianne and Edward Dozier with their children in Baguio City, Philippines, 1960. The child on the left is Migué; Anya is on the right. (Dozier Collection, D-34, Arizona State Museum, University of Arizona)

information about rice planting, ritual sacrifices to the ancestors, attitudes toward illness, peace pact celebrations, gossip, and care of children. He also made notes on stories, the local language, genealogies, and the names of municipal officials. One notebook entry described an incident intended to warn him about the dangers he would face if he continued his journey past Lubuagan. "[They] filled me with wild tales of how unsafe—Kalingas in Mabaca will kill by witchcraft etc. poison people esp. old women who have had no children—believe to lengthen lives by so doing. Interesting how suspicious mt. folk are of some people a few kilometers beyond. Actually [there are] some friendly Kalinga everywhere and strangers particularly are safe" (EPD4.3, Lubuagan field notebook, October 15, 1959). Dozier was aware that the Ilongots had killed William Jones at the turn of the century, but after dutifully recording his hosts' concern for his physical safety, he continued his travels.

Fortunately, language proved to be no barrier for Dozier in the Philippines, because so many Filipinos, including Kalingas, spoke English. Although he occasionally used interpreters in Kalinga villages, he noted that even Kalinga elders "frequently spoke English, so that communication was not a problem at any time" (Dozier 1966b:xiii). Dozier could speak Spanish, but as Fred Eggan observed about Philippine life, "Spanish didn't help you very much" (Fred Eggan, interview, May 12, 1988).

Dozier's Kalinga consultants were elders in the villages for data on traditional customs and, to some extent, acculturated Kalinga college students in Baguio City for information on contemporary conditions (Dozier 1966b:xii). The latter also served as his guides and facilitated contacts in the villages. In a letter to a friend of Eggan's, a Philippine scholar called "Scotty" (possibly William H. Scott), Dozier explained his use of informants and student helpers. There were parallels between the Baguio students and Dozier himself during his college days, when he worked with Sergeant and Hill at Santa Clara:

> My information on social organization, agriculture, religion, head hunting (warfare) all come from old informants—indeed the only place I could have gotten a good picture of these aspects since there is so much change going on in these areas. The modern situation is drawn from informants who are products of the modern Philippine school system for the most part—not necessarily young. I rarely asked or used information supplied by the Baguio students who lived, worked and acted as guides for me. These latter were extremely helpful in getting typing done and other aid in getting my notes together and through them I met the older people in the villages who supplied the information that forms the bulk of my study. (EPD4.1, Dozier to Scotty [no surname], November 8, 1962)

As a general field practice, he did not pay his consultants (although there were exceptions); rather, he "compensated them with gifts" (Dozier 1966b:xv). These gifts took many forms, including photographs that Dozier took of their families and his agreeing to give speeches at peace pact ceremonies and school graduations.

Conducting ethnographic research on the Kalingas challenged Dozier's understandings of culture and society. Initially he responded to Kalinga society through the filter of familiar Pueblo Indian customs. Making a comparison between the Kalingas and the Pueblos as an exercise in "point and counterpoint," he wrote about his first impressions: "Kindred loyalty and trust as they operate among the Kalinga have largely eliminated suspicion and distrust within the group. My own Pueblo background made it difficult to accept this state of affairs among the Kalinga for a long time. I kept looking for the kind of damaging, back-biting gossip (although rarely in the open) which characterizes intra-group relations among the Pueblos" (Dozier 1966b:188). He also "expected to find evidences of witchcraft and sorcery among the Kalinga":

> Among the Pueblo and elsewhere, witchcraft appears where close neighbors are distrusted and feared. The Kalinga vent their hostilities on the enemy, or did until recently, while most of their fears and anxieties are bound up with supernaturals. Intra-group wrongs and offenses are immediately challenged and brought up openly before regional leaders and resolved as kindred or kindred segment responsibilities. These factors undoubtedly explain why witchcraft, which is born of fear, distrust, and suspicion of closely interacting individuals (often near relatives), has not been a problem among the Kalinga. (Dozier 1966b:189)

For the first time in his field experiences Dozier was permitted to take notes on his observations in public, something he could never do when researching Pueblo societies. He was also able to name and acknowledge his major informants without fear of reprisals against them (Dozier 1966b:xiii). He happily related: "This was a delightful experience after my work among the Pueblo Indians of the southwestern United States, where the ethnographer is always suspect and note-taking is taboo except when the complete confidence of an informant has been gained, and then only in a place where the ethnographer is alone with his informant" (Dozier 1966b:xiv).

Another striking contrast he observed between the Kalingas and the Pueblos lay in their very different attitudes toward anthropological field photography. Neither the Arizona Tewas nor the Hopis allowed anyone to make photographs or drawings of their ceremonial dances. Moreover, any individual Pueblo who was photographed might feel betrayed to find his or her image in an anthropological publication, considering it a breach of trust by the anthropologist. A published portrait might create gossip and raise local suspicions that the person had given away secret information. Field relations might then suffer if the anthropologist was no longer welcome in the community. Dozier tried to explain these cultural constraints on the use of Arizona Tewa photographs to his book editor and fellow UCLA graduate, George Spindler: "Unfortunately the only pictures I have of Hano adults are close friends and people deep in religious affairs. I could not return to Hano if I used the pictures and they'll get to see them I'm sure" (EPD4.1, Dozier to Spindler, March 29, 1965).

Although Dozier had taken photographs of the Arizona Tewas, he was careful about publishing the images; he preferred that editors use museum photographs taken by others (EPD4.1, Dozier to Spindler, May 15, 1965). As much as possible he selected photographs from museum collections, such as those of the Arizona State Museum and the Smithsonian Institution (EPD4.1, Dozier to Spindler, April 29, 1959). Generally, the work of professional photographers illustrated his Pueblo books. Dozier explained to his editors: "I hope you can get along with the pictures I supplied—even this may bring on a negative reaction, but all except one were taken by Milton Snow hence the blame may not fall on me!" (EPD4.1, Dozier to Spindler, March 29, 1965).

In contrast to the Pueblos, the Kalingas had no cultural objections to Dozier's taking photographs. Using a thirty-five-millimeter camera he took numerous pictures of Kalinga cultural activities and the environment. In a letter to Fred Eggan he men-

Figure 9. Edward Dozier (front row, third from the left) sitting inconspicuously among the Kalinga peacekeepers in Salegseg, Balbalan municipal district, Philippines, April 1960. (Dozier Collection, D-23, Arizona State Museum, University of Arizona)

tioned: "I just came back from attending two peacepact celebrations.... Never did so much walking in my life! ... I was flattered by being the 'guest speaker' in both places and being honored by dancing with the Poswoy peacepact holder (a woman) and one from Asiga also a woman. I took pictures like mad and I hope some of them turn out" (EPD4.1, Dozier to Eggan, May 10, 1960).

Recording his visits to mountain villages, he often made portraits of Kalinga mothers and children, perhaps reflecting his own family life and his wife's professional interest in child development. Sometimes he had other people take photographs of him—waiting at a busy bus depot, dancing with women at a peace pact celebration in Bolo, wearing a comfortable plaid shirt and rolled-up blue jeans, picnicking with young men near the Soltan River in Posway, posing on a wooden bridge in Ableg with scenic thatched houses in the distance, and sitting among men in Naway whom he so resembled that it is difficult to identify the anthropologist among the locals (Edward Dozier photographic collection, Arizona State Museum, University of Arizona).

Fieldwork in the mountains of northern Luzon was physically demanding, but in order for Dozier to gain an understanding of Kalinga society, it was imperative that he travel as much as possible. In his 1967 ethnography he explained:

> To understand the broad patterns of Kalinga life, a field researcher must cover considerable territory in an extremely rugged and mountainous terrain. The scattered residence pattern which disperses families of a kindred into different hamlets brings about considerable mobility of the regional population. . . . During the dry season mobility is accentuated and travel is extended interregionally; anywhere from three to ten peace pact celebrations might be visited over a period of three months by the Kalinga themselves. . . . I became a part of this pattern of mobility and went along with the Kalinga to regional festivals and the popular interregional peace pact celebrations. (Dozier 1967a:vii)

On one four-day trip in October 1959 through the mountain provinces of northern Luzon, Dozier encountered a geography dramatically different from that of the American Southwest. Traveling with a Kalinga student, he took a bus from Baguio City to Bontoc, a town about seventy miles north. There the two stayed overnight in the relatively "plush comfort" of a Protestant missionary's house. Then they took a "long and bumpy ride" on another bus, past rice terraces, to the town of Lubuagan, where Dozier slept "on a hard bed with a single cover" at the student's family home. From there the student's brother-in-law became Dozier's traveling companion as he journeyed to the heavily populated region of Selegseg, spending the night at a Roman Catholic convent. The next day the men hiked fifteen kilometers on a "trail rough and steep" through various *sitios* (places of residence, or barrios) of the northern Kalingas in the region of Mabaca. He stayed at a house for "two or three days [to] observe, take a few notes and pictures and then return" (EPD4.3, Lubuagan field notes, October 15, 1959).

It was the "trail rough and steep" from Selegseg to Mabaca, in a rain forest environment of rapid rivers and deep canyons, that tested Dozier most arduously:

> The Saltan River . . . is swift and deep . . . clear, beautiful water—a hanging, shaky foot bridge spans the river. Across the river, the trail splits into a "short cut" and the regular, longer trail. Foolishly perhaps I consented to the guides' suggestion we take the short cut which climbed up the side of the mountain almost perpendicularly over wet slippery rocks. The boys all in their teens or rounding twenty scampered up the . . . side despite their bare feet (or perhaps because of it). The trip was too fast for me though I tried to keep up for a while. The hearty breakfast began to act up on me and I lost it about half way up—with attendant illness. But a wait of a few hours helped to get me over the worst of it and we resumed our journey—the trail seemed to be forever climbing. Three men carrying heavy bundles of window materials caught up with us and joined us, but since I had to call halt periodically they finally left us and proceeded on ahead. . . .
>
> About 1 p.m. we finally reached the summit—after a terrific grueling climb consuming almost six hours. The descent was almost straight down over a gravelly trail with frequent boulders—soon we were in terraced rice fields—but the descent never slackened in difficulties. It also began to rain and this added to our difficulties. Incidentally the baggage was being carried by the boys—one suitcase weighing I suspect close to 50 lbs., a hand bag of perhaps 20 lbs. and other odds and ends up to about 100 lbs. They seemed not be to bothered by all this weight and nimbly came down the Mt. (and up before it)—how they can stand the rough trail on bare feet remains an amazing thing to me. (EPD4.3, Convento, Salegseg notes, October 15–17, 1959)

Although the journey was fatiguing for the forty-three-year-old anthropologist, it gave him the opportunity to make firsthand observations. He developed contacts with potential informants who would follow him back to Baguio City for interviews. He also participated in a feast for a newborn child and ate carabao, or water buffalo, meat for the first time.

As he interviewed informants and observed village life, Dozier collected oral and written histories in order to reconstruct the migrations of populations, the diffusion of metal technology and languages, the effects of a boarding school education on traditional life, and the evolving role of native clergy. From his personal experiences Dozier could identify with the younger, acculturated Kalingas. And he could relate to the similarities between the colonial histories of the Philippines and the Pueblo Southwest—the influence of Spanish missions, residents' flight to the mountains to escape oppression, the suppression of native traditions by the American military, the introduction of wage work into a subsistence economy, and the establishment of schools for native children.

Dozier particularly focused on the peace pact as a mechanism for local arbitration of disputes in the absence of headhunting. According to his analysis, the traditional status of the headhunter as warrior had been culturally reinterpreted through the interregional peace pact system. The Reverend Miguel Seys, a missionary from Salegseg, told Dozier that a warrior named Gaddawan had introduced the idea of a peace pact to stop the killings and increase the population and wealth through regional alliances (EPD4.1, Seys to Dozier, May 15, 1963). The Kalingas deliberately ended headhunting and created cultural mechanisms such as arbitration to replace the former practice. Their peace pacts were regarded as binding legal contracts. Over time, these oral agreements were transcribed into written documents that recorded the distinct interregional political and legal histories of the peace pact holders (Dozier 1966b).

Dozier's Kalinga field notes are rich in peace pact histories. He made detailed lists of current peace pact holders and the regions covered by the pacts, and he explained how the highly valued pacts were inherited from generation to generation. He constructed chronologies showing when the political alliances had been initi-

Figure 10. Edward Dozier on a bridge in Albeg, Lubuagan municipal district, Philippines, 1959–60. Photography became a new resource in Dozier's ethnographic fieldwork in the Philippines. Many illustrations in his 1966 book *Mountain Arbiters: The Changing Life of a Philippine Hill People* were his own black-and-white photographs. (Dozier Collection, D-36P, Arizona State Museum, University of Arizona)

ated and renewed. He compiled the regional profiles and published them as legal and cultural histories in an appendix to his 1996 ethnography (Dozier 1966b:269–82). His data revealed the diversity of peace pacts, the years in which they had been initiated, and the names and locations of the individuals who had inherited them through specific kinship networks in each region. Dozier's chronicle of peace pact histories comprised original source material for regional municipal districts from 1902 to 1960—a significant resource for researchers studying Kalinga politics, economics, law, or kinship. Fred Eggan regarded the quality of Dozier's rich data on peace pacts as "excellent" (EPD4.1, Eggan to Dozier, November 17, 1959).

In looking at his original research problem—the comparison of social and cultural differences between the northern and southern Kalingas—Dozier employed the historical method. He did not dispute R.F. Barton's thesis that the differences stemmed from the two groups' respective subsistence economies, but he emphasized that the groups' dissimilar contact histories were also significant variables:

> Investigations of past conditions by questioning informants and examining historical documents revealed that differences between the two groups of Kalinga were also profoundly affected by historical circumstances. The Northern Kalinga [were] influenced by Spanish penetration in the Abra and the Ilocos lowlands to the west. This influence came indirectly by contact with such groups as the Tinguian and Illocano, particularly the latter, who directly experienced the modification of their culture by Spanish civil and religious administration. On the other hand, proximity to and contact with the complex irrigated rice cultivators of the Bontoc and Ifugao influenced the Southern Kalinga in another direction. It has been impossible, therefore, to isolate completely the economic from the historic variables, in accounting for differences between the two groups. Both of these factors, economic and historical, are intricately involved, and both may be considered as causal agents in explaining the differences between the Southern and Northern Kalinga. (Dozier 1966b:6–9)

Dozier also attempted to demystify the historical practice of headhunting and interpret the Kalingas' violent behavior in the context of their contemporary value of "venting anger on Others" to maintain village harmony (Dozier 1966b:197–237). By concentrating on community values he succeeded in taking the "foreignness" out of a seemingly exotic practice. As an anthropologist he contextualized headhunting culturally and historically, revealing it to have been a culturally normal and pragmatic practice for Kalingas in the past.

Perhaps his cultural interpretation of headhunting was best expressed in a letter he wrote to a former student in which he commented on the death of William Jones at the hands of Ilongots with whom Jones had enjoyed a good field relationship:

> Headhunting in the Philippines is among one's own kind,... and a stranger unless he is an outright bungler is perfectly safe. The only American (a Fox Indian from Iowa!) William Jones was unfortunately killed by the Ilongot. Anthropologists say that on the very last day, on his way back to Manila and then from there to take a boat to America, the Ilongots slew him and took his head. It was an honor! These fierce headhunters liked Jones so much that they wanted his spirit to be with them always. (EPD4.1, Dozier to Bob [no surname], January 30, 1969)

Despite Dozier's ethnographic information on headhunting and the richness of his peace pact data, neither of his two published ethnographies of the Kalingas ever became a well-cited reference in Philippine studies (William Longacre, interview, March 29, 1989; see also Kaut 1967; LeBar 1968; Longacre and Skibo 1994). Dozier himself acknowledged the limitations that time and travel constraints imposed on his fieldwork methods (Dozier 1966b). In a book review, Michiko Takaki (1969), a Yale University anthropologist who specialized in southern Kalinga communities, pointed out serious problems in Dozier's comparative approach. She criticized several aspects of the 1966 ethnography: Dozier's reliance on English instead of learning a field language; the absence of clear criteria for his regional classifications; his lack of sufficient data for sampling and for determining basic structural relationships within subcultures; and his failure to present quantitative data and analyses for regional economics. She also contested Dozier's representation that Kalinga ethnographic information was fully accessible, believing instead that a category of knowledge existed that was "vigorously protected by them against leakage to those outside a closed circuit" (Takaki 1969:516).

Robert Maher (1968), writing in *American Anthropologist,* took a more positive view of Dozier's companion publication, *The Kalinga of Northern Luzon, Philippines* (1967a). He acknowledged the pedagogical value for undergraduate anthropology students of Dozier's case study of a famous peace pact institution. Yet like Takaki he saw the weakness in Dozier's regional comparisons—an area that Dozier himself recognized needed additional field study in the future. Whatever the merits of Dozier's work, few later ethnographers working in the region have regarded it as central to their studies (e.g., Rosaldo 1980).

In the context of the paradox of the American Indian anthropologist, however, the significance of the Kalinga ethnographies lies not in their cultural description but in Dozier's achievement of having studied the anthropological other as an outsider anthropologist. His fieldwork in the Philippines broadened his anthropological ability to analyze variations in social institutions and qualified him to expand his teaching in the academy into another culture area. He had successfully reached beyond the borders of Pueblo Indian anthropology through his direct participation in the academic discourse of Southeast Asian studies. Now, having accomplished this goal, it was time for him to return home to the American Southwest.

Leadership in American Indian Studies

For all of us [American Indians] there has always been the problem of "second class citizenship." This has expressed itself in the deprivation of full rights as citizens and the nagging and vexing problem of discrimination. Here our problems are not unique, for we share them with other ethnic minority groups. . . . [In other cases] our problems are different and demand different solutions, since they arise out of our historical occupation and attachment to the American soil and its ancient heritage.
—Edward Dozier, keynote address at
the American Indian Chicago Conference, 1961

Dozier's attachment to his ancestral Pueblo heritage brought him back to the Southwest in 1960. He joined the Department of Anthropology at the University of Arizona (UA) in Tucson as a professor of anthropology in September, at an annual salary of $8,500. He worked there until his early death in May 1971.

Department chair Emil Haury, who hired Dozier, explained to the university's administration the importance of Dozier's position within the department's four-field approach to anthropology:

Dr. Dozier's areas of specialization are linguistics and cultural anthropology. . . . he will be able to provide the linguistics training required of our majors and at the same time emphasize and strengthen the relationship which should exist between linguistics and cultural anthropology.

In addition to the fact that we believe him to be ideally trained for our program and he is a thoroughly competent scholar, we approve of the fact that his background is

Indian, Santa Clara Pueblo, New Mexico. An Indian leader of one of our Arizona tribes asked me last summer, "What inspiration is there for our boys to get a college education?" We believe that Dr. Dozier's appointment will have a wholesome effect apart from the contributions he will make as a scholar. (UA Special Collections biographical file, Edward Dozier, Haury to Dean Roy, December 10, 1958)

Haury's words were prophetic. Dozier joined the UA faculty at a time of civil rights ferment, and he fully supported the offering of greater educational opportunities to American Indians and other minority students. In 1961 he delivered the keynote address at a historic meeting known as the American Indian Chicago Conference, organized by the anthropologist Sol Tax at the University of Chicago (EPD4.4). He spoke candidly about racial discrimination and the problems facing minority Americans. His words in 1961 prefigured the emergence of ethnic studies programs at American universities over the next two decades. This was a movement in which Dozier, as an indigenous scholar, would soon become a leading figure. His tribal identity, coupled with his reputation as a senior scholar at a major research university, lent him authority as an advocate for minorities in higher education. He soon found himself in a position of power to significantly influence the structure of academic affairs.

The emergence of American Indian Studies (AIS) programs was an epiphenomenon of the national civil rights and affirmative action movements in the late 1960s. At universities across the nation, students were protesting for minority civil rights through educational reform, claiming that the current college curriculum was ethnocentric. They petitioned for changes that would acknowledge their historical, linguistic, and cultural differences and their contributions to American society. Students insisted on a curriculum that addressed relevant contemporary issues, and they demanded a voice in institutional decision making. Overall, theirs was a revolution for structural reform in higher education with the objective of repositioning minorities away from the margins and into the mainstream of academic life.

For American Indians specifically, the pan-Indian movement was front-page news. High-profile vents such as the occupation of Alcatraz Island by American Indians in 1969 and the seizure of the town of Wounded Knee, South Dakota, by members of the American Indian Movement in 1973 created a new public awareness of historical inequities and the contemporary dilemmas of native people—including their exclusion from higher education (Deloria and Lytle 1969). The universities that responded to these pressing needs were those located in places with large American Indian populations—specifically, states with tribal reservations (Arizona, New Mexico, Minnesota) and urban areas heavily affected by federal termination policies (Los Angeles).

Land grant colleges, with their legislative mandates to serve state residents, including American Indians, were uniquely responsive. These universities began a movement toward new, interdisciplinary ethnic studies programs, among them programs focused particularly on American Indians. The early programs were called by various names—American Indian Studies, Native American Studies, Alaskan Native Studies. In 1969 Dozier commented that this educational reform movement was a response to the "clamor for programs on American Indian studies in . . . our major Western U.S. institutions. . . . both Berkeley and San Francisco State have plans for starting American Indian programs" (EPD4.1, Dozier to Bill [Willard], August 17, 1969).

The emergence of AIS programs during the 1960s and 1970s did not take place without institutional struggles over how native rights were to be represented within the academy. A fundamental issue was whether such programs would focus on the education *of* American Indians or on education *about* American Indians. That is, would the AIS program and curriculum serve tribal students and native faculty, or would it be structured for a broad student body (Henry 1972)?

At the University of Arizona, as at other universities around the country, this debate involved diverse constituencies—faculty members, university administrators, tribal leaders, students, and philanthropic organizations. Each group of stakeholders had its own policy, vision, and vested interest in the future of AIS. Charitable foundations were the dominant powers in defining American Indian higher education, through their review, acceptance, rejection, or modification of universities' grant proposals. The foundations' decisions, based upon their own policies and financial guidelines, were not insignificant in their effects on the initial designs of AIS programs.

The issue was particularly controversial for academic departments. Bundling existing classes into a cross-listed offering for all students was the simplest alternative. It would require departments to make only minor changes, yet foundation money would allow them to hire new faculty members—Indian or non-Indian—to teach courses on American Indian subjects. Setting up a separate, specialized program in competition with existing departments for funding dollars and prestige was quite a different scenario, one that threatened the balance of power among traditional disciplines, centers, and schools on campus. Consequently, every university arbitrated its own unique program, reflecting its local political and economic environment.

The University of Arizona in Tucson, a leader at the time, had begun creating academic and support programs to meet American Indians' needs as early as the 1950s. As a land grant college, it had been created by the Arizona territorial legislature in 1885 with a mandate to provide services to the citizens of the state. By the 1970s almost 110,000 American Indians, representing seventeen tribes, lived in Arizona. One quarter of the state's land base consisted of federal trust land for twenty-three reservations (EPD4.6, UA proposal to Ford Foundation, ca. 1970). The university, therefore, had a special obligation to create initiatives that would serve Arizona's Indian population.

In 1952, eight years before Dozier's arrival, UA established a Bureau of Ethnic Research under the direction of anthropologist William Kelly. It conducted applied anthropology projects in economics, education, and demographics and dealt "almost exclusively in Arizona Indian affairs" (EPD4.6, UA proposal to Ford Foundation, ca. 1970). In 1958 UA president Richard A. Harvill appointed an Indian Advisory Committee (IAC) for university-tribal relations, initially funded by the Lilly Foundation and chaired by Edward Spicer.

In 1968 Harvill created yet another campuswide committee dedicated to improving the university's relationship with the state's American Indian tribes. The impetus for forming it came from an external source, an Arizona tribal chairman. As a university report explained:

> The organization was stimulated by a letter from Clarence Wesley, Tribal Chairman of the San Carlos Apache Tribe. He was primarily concerned with Indian educational problems and what the University could do to solve some of these problems. At this time Dr. Harvill appointed the Committee on Indian Affairs. Some of the results of this Committee were the appointment of an Indian Student Advisor; training seminars in Indian Art sponsored by the Rockefeller Foundation; and annual training conferences for Indian judges. (AIS office files, Indian Advisory Committee Minutes, September 26, 1968)

The role of the Indian student advisor was critical in addressing Indian educational problems because it bridged reservation and university life. The adviser was to "assist Indian students in their transition from a home environment into the University community through counseling at both the academic and personal adjustment level, through soliciting wider campus involvement in the affairs of the American Indian student, and through support of student-initiated efforts to develop programs of their own" (EPD4.6, UA proposal to Ford Foundation, ca. 1970).

The growth and diversity of American Indian programs at UA also motivated Harvill to create a new position, a coordinator of Indian programs, who would report to the vice president for university relations. In 1968 he hired applied anthropologist Gordon Krutz as coordinator and Emory Sekaquaptewa, a Hopi who had graduated from the UA law school, as his assistant. Harvill also established an advisory committee of deans and department heads who counseled him on policy regarding the educational needs of tribes in relation to university resources.

It is noteworthy that all Indian programs and personnel at UA, including the Bureau of Ethnic Research, the Indian student advisor, the coordinator of Indian programs, and eventually the new American Indian Studies program, came under the umbrella of the Department of Anthropology. It was chaired by Emil Haury until 1964 and then by Raymond Thompson until 1980. It was Edward Dozier's home department.

Dozier himself served as the Indian student advisor during the sabbatical leave of Harry Getty in 1961–62 (EPD4.1, Dozier to Harvill, March 1, 1961). He oversaw thirty-five students and also served as a sponsor for the campus Amerind Club (Department of Anthropology, UA Biennial Catalogue, 1963–64, 1964–65). He wrote reports on American Indian academic issues for the university's biennial catalogs for 1963–64 and 1964–65, noting, "There seems to be a growing interest among Indians in the programs of higher education at the University of Arizona, to which the Indian Student Advisor has responded by personally addressing various groups at conferences and meetings" (UA Biennial Catalog, 1963–65, Appendix 6, Special Collections, UA Library). Statistical records for the 1968–69 fiscal year state that approximately 187 resident American Indian students attended UA as full-time undergraduates.

During Edward Spicer's sabbatical leave in 1963–64, Harvill asked Dozier to serve as chair of the university's Committee on Indian Affairs. Again he was a temporary replacement for a non-Indian scholar. But that pattern would soon change. Dozier was elected chair of the Indian Advisory Committee in 1968, and two years later, in 1970, he would rise to the top leadership position of American Indian Studies.

Accomplished American Indian scholars were rare assets for educational institutions in the 1960s. Finding qualified native scholars to direct innovative American Indian studies programs became a priority for both universities and foundations. In political and economic contexts, an American Indian scholar brought instant legitimacy and authority to a nascent cultural program. For example, in 1971 the Newberry Library in Chicago applied for a large National Endowment for the Humanities grant to establish an American Indian Research Center. D'Arcy McNickle's biographer explained the selection of McNickle as the center's first program director: "If the grant was received, the new center would need as a spokesperson someone who could encourage the white establishment to provide matching funds and at the same time establish the center's credibility with both the scholarly and Indian communities.... McNickle, as both an Indian and a scholar, was more than qualified to serve in this dual capacity" (Parker 1992:240).

The political climate surrounding ethnic identity, civil rights, and affirmative action was changing dramatically in the United States, and universities reflected the revolution of social reform. The academic paradox of the Indian scholar was shifting from the shadows to the spotlight as universities searched for native leaders in American Indian Studies initiatives. As a result, the modest and self-effacing Edward Dozier became identified by the university and foundations as a desirable asset. A colleague reminisced about the attitudes of the times:

> I don't think that anybody afforded him any special status or anything . . . with one exception. And that is when it looked as if there might be money available for an American Indian Studies program. Then inevitably you had to look around for an Indian as your front person on the whole thing. And Ed's the one who picked up the ball. So you know then he was cast heavily in the role of, in an Indian role, as giving legitimacy to requests for money from the Ford Foundation for an Indian program to be headed by an Indian. (Bernard Fontana, interview, May 29, 1991)

Dozier was neither self-promoting nor competitive. It was others' political perceptions of him and his inherent "legitimacy" as a

Pueblo Indian and a nationally recognized scholar that created for him a leadership position in university affairs. Universities' desire for academic programs with native leadership opened a new market for minorities in higher education. Dozier received unsolicited attention as others identified him as a top candidate to head new, emerging American Indian Studies programs. The university's decision to promote a native scholar, coupled with his own personal and professional commitment to improving Indian higher education, made a powerful combination, although each party was motivated by distinctly different values.

Other major universities attempted to recruit Dozier. In 1965 he was approached by Arizona State University in nearby Tempe, but the overture failed "because of strong administrative support [by UA] in adjusting [his] teaching and research responsibilities" (Annual Report, UA Department of Anthropology, 1965–66). In 1969 the University of Minnesota offered him "an appointment as Professor and Chairman of the Department of American Indian Studies at a salary of $23,500 for the academic year" (EPD4.1, Ziebarth to Dozier, October 23, 1969). The job came with the rank of full professor in the Department of Anthropology. Dozier declined the attractive offer; at the time, he was recovering from surgery and remained in Arizona to convalesce (Dozier family interview, November 7, 1988).

Although Dozier was finding himself increasingly drawn into the AIS movement, he remained exceptionally productive in his academic work during his years at UA. From the mid-1960s through 1970 he published four books on the Kalingas and the Pueblos (1966a, 1966b, 1967a, 1970a). He wrote numerous articles on diverse topics: Pueblo factionalism (1966c), Pueblo self-government (1969a), prehistory and Pueblo society (1965b, 1970b), Southwestern culture contact (1965a), American Indian alcoholism (1966f), linguistic acculturation studies (1966e, 1967b), and the pedagogical issue of teachers of Indian students (1969c). By 1969 he had begun to express an interest in studying contemporary urban Indians in the San Francisco Bay area, but he was unable to pursue it because of ill health (EPD4.1, Dozier to Bill [Willard], August 17, 1969).

During a sabbatical year in 1967-68 Dozier researched what was to become his most important intellectual legacy—his ethnology of Southwestern Pueblo cultures, *The Pueblo Indians of North America* (1970a). Of all his works, this book has been the most widely cited and used in classroom instruction. With the financial support of a Guggenheim fellowship, he assembled a systematic study of Pueblo prehistory, colonial relations, contemporary conditions, languages, and governments. As he wrote in the preface, it was "the result of a lifetime spent among the Pueblos" (Dozier 1970a:xi). Although one anthropologist criticized the accuracy of his Zuni generalizations (Tedlock 1972), on the whole the book was well received in the discipline and in American Indian Studies in Dozier's time, as it still is today.

Dozier's later years at UA were also a time of institutional recognition for him. The Association on American Indian Affairs elected him second vice president in 1968. The Ford Foundation offered him a position on its committee that awarded fellowships for dissertations in ethnic studies (EPD4.1, Scanlon to Dozier, January 19, 1971). The American Association for the Advancement of Science offered him membership on a new "Committee on Minorities in Science" (EPD4.1, Dozier to William Bevan, January 22, 1971). Dozier accepted both offers, as well as chairmanship of the American Anthropological Association's Ethics Committee.

In 1969, while writing his cross-cultural synthesis of the Pueblo Indians, Dozier was named head of the Committee on Indian Affairs, a high-profile university position. In that capacity he received funding from the Rockefeller Foundation to conduct a survey of all American Indian Studies programs in the United States (Annual Report, UA Department of Anthropology, 1969-70). The survey data would inform the design of UA's program.

Incorporating the survey results with UA's prior experience in several Indian programs, Dozier and his colleagues on the committee—Raymond Thompson (chair of the Department of

Figure 11. Edward P. Dozier, professor of anthropology, at the University of Arizona, 1967. (Dozier Collection, 14903, Arizona State Museum, University of Arizona; Helga Teiwes, photographer)

Anthropology and director of the Arizona State Museum), Bernard Fontana (curator of ethnology, Arizona State Museum), Tom Weaver (Bureau of Ethnic Research), Gordon Krutz (coordinator of Indian programs), Emory Sekaquaptewa (co-coordinator of Indian programs), and Edward Spicer (former chair of the Indian Advisory Committee)—designed a concept for an interdisciplinary

AIS program. It was to be "the first of its kind in the nation, with the mission and goals of strengthening Indian-related curriculum and expanding the number of American Indian faculty members and students at the University. Dr. Edward P. Dozier, a Tewa from the Santa Clara Pueblo and an anthropologist of considerable international reputation, organized this initiative" (American Indian Studies faculty 1991:11). Early in 1970 the University of Arizona appointed Dozier its first chair of American Indian Studies. He was charged with transforming a university initiative from concept on paper to actual academic program on campus.

The first hurdle was getting funding. Securing seed money to underwrite the program's initial costs was a major responsibility for Dozier and the committee. They applied to the Carnegie and Ford Foundations for grants, proposing a program that centered on the needs of Indian students rather than on faculty. They took the position that AIS should focus on the education *of* American Indians, not solely on education *about* Indians.

In the Carnegie proposal, Dozier described how an AIS program would increase the number of American Indian college students at UA: "Launching of this program will enable a number of young Indians to take advantage of higher education. At present, university and/or college educational opportunities are avoided by Indians because of anxieties in facing a maze of students, faculty and administrators. . . . We believe this project will make the possibility of a university experience less frightening and, hopefully, attractive to bright, young Indians on isolated reservations" (EPD4.1, Dozier to Finberg, October 15, 1970).

In their first—unsuccessful—proposal to the Ford Foundation, Dozier and the committee stressed the need for high school counseling and recruitment, scholarship aid, and specialized training for Indian students. They wanted not only to increase the number of Indian students at the university but also to improve their retention (Bernard Fontana, interview, May 29, 1991). Hiring five "student-counselors" would facilitate the recruitment of Indians from Tucson area high schools. The intention was that "university Indian students . . . would visit the Indian students on a regular basis" and serve as college role models and liaisons" (EPD4.6, undated Ford Foundation proposal, 8). Dozier and Spicer designed this social infrastructure to bridge the cultural problems of Indian students as they made the transition from reservation to university (Bernard Fontana, interview, 29 May 1991). Five such students would take a special class in guidance and counseling and would apply those skills at Indian high schools. The Indian student-counselors would also serve as big brothers and big sisters "to help the newcomers make an effective transition from reservation life to campus life" (EPD4.6, undated Ford Foundation proposal, 10). This system would benefit the high school student, the college student, and the university in recruitment and retention.

The committee's first proposal to the Ford Foundation also recommended that the university hold summer workshops for Indian students on linguistics and ethnohistory. Dozier's vision of training native linguists and serving tribal communities, although never realized, was one of revolutionary change in relations between anthropologists and American Indians:

> *Summer Workshop in Linguistics and Ethnohistory.* There is an increasing emphasis in anthropology on the value of the knowledge that an Indian speaker has of his language and culture. Unfortunately, though, few Indians can communicate this knowledge to others. Our workshop is an attempt to make linguists and ethnohistorians out of Indian students so that they can use their native ability in their language and culture to enrich all of anthropology. We believe that this approach has real advantages over the traditional one of anthropologists attempting, but almost never succeeding, in gaining native proficiency in another language and culture. The Indian who has been taught to be an analyst of what he knows can speak with the authority that no one else can equal. Not only can Indians communicate their knowledge of their culture as insiders, but with this training, they can begin to enjoy the recognition and status that has only been given to anthropologists in the past.

We specifically plan on recruiting ten Indian students who are bilingual from the tribal reservations in Arizona. We will select them on the basis of recommendations from their tribal councils as well as their potential to benefit from our training. Each student will attend five weeks of classes. He will attend each morning with Anglo students a course in introductory cultural anthropology and one in introductory linguistics. Each afternoon he will be given tutorial help in linguistics and ethnohistorical techniques to make sure that he understands the material presented and can apply it in his situation.

When he has finished the workshop, he should be able to begin an analysis of his language and culture. We expect he will either go on in his studies and become a professional anthropologist or serve his tribe in some other scholarly way. (EPD4.6, undated Ford Foundation proposal, 11–12)

Dozier and the committee additionally requested financial aid for "qualified college-age Indians" and urban Indians to attend the University of Arizona. They also proposed the hiring of "faculty members of American Indian descent" and "two outstanding linguists" in American Indian languages. Funds for Arizona State Museum library acquisitions in American Indian materials (mostly tribal and federal documents) were requested as well. Altogether, Dozier, as principal investigator, asked for a five-year grant totaling $1 million.

Despite Dozier's professional status and leadership, the Ford and Carnegie Foundations rejected the concept of a program centered on American Indian students. Both organizations turned down the committee's proposals. A Ford Foundation administrator wrote to Dozier with formal notification in October 1970: "I have received your proposal to assist prospective American Indian students to attend colleges and universities. Although your project design is very worthwhile, I regret that the Ford Foundation is unable to be of assistance to you" (EPD4.6, S. Oppenheimer to Dozier, October 21, 1970). As another Ford staff member later explained to Raymond Thompson, the foundation explicitly refused to fund specialized training and support for American Indian students, "even though we recognize how important they are to what you are trying to do in the field of American Indian studies" (EPD4.1, Scanlon to Thompson, March 25, 1971).

In response, Dozier and his committee began to draft a revised proposal. With regret, they dropped the funding package for Indian students—a serious setback for the like-minded committee members. In their second grant application, they centered the program on the faculty. They requested funding to hire scholars who specialized in American Indians—not necessarily American Indians themselves—who would be placed in traditional academic departments rather than in an independent program. Shifting away from their prior aim of serving American Indian students in higher education, they proposed an interdisciplinary program for a general student body interested in cultural diversity.

The new proposal reflected a growing consensus at the time that neither Indian nor non-Indian students would find a degree from a stand-alone American Indian Studies program to be marketable. Dozier agreed with this appraisal, as one colleague recalled:

> Ed was concerned, [from] the purely practical point of view, that if we started an Indian studies program, [if] it was self-contained and . . . led to some kind of degree called Indian Studies that nobody would be able to sell it. Once you got such a degree, what would you do with it? In the real world, it wasn't going to be a very practical kind of thing to do. Then, what he believed in was, I think, that you're better off by having Indians as role models all over the campus. . . . Ed felt that what was needed was more Indian faculty members to let the Indian students know that they, too, could do whatever. (Bernard Fontana, interview, May 29, 1991)

This interdisciplinary sentiment partly explained the university's decision to reapply to the Ford Foundation for a program that would cross-list courses on American Indian topics across the university. Under the new plan, the university would hire American Indian faculty and place them in existing departments that offered degrees in standard disciplines. It was an easy institutional accommodation because it would neither change nor challenge the structure or internal power relations of the university. Instead, it would enrich the diversity of the existing faculty and the curriculum. Raymond Thompson explained this arrangement in a letter to Roger Buffalohead, who had accepted the directorship of the AIS program at the University of Minnesota after Dozier declined it. Thompson advocated an interdisciplinary approach to AIS that would utilize "the many courses that have long been taught on American Indian topics" (EPD 4.6, Thompson to Buffalohead, December 30, 1970).

In retrospect, establishing AIS as a campuswide interdisciplinary program was a pragmatic and conservative course of action with good intent. As Dozier remarked later, UA was "dependent on the Ford grant for launching the entire American Indian program" (EPD4.1, Dozier to J. Muskrat, April 26, 1971). The compromise plan was a first step in a slow trend toward institutional change. Because it would not conflict with existing academic relations, it would receive interdepartmental support. The new hires, it was hoped, would inject American Indian perspectives into disciplines where they did not yet exist. As the committee explained it to the Ford Foundation: "The purpose of such faculty additions is to give American Indian scholars a 'home' in University departmental disciplines in which they have been trained, simultaneously offering their courses for credit in the American Indian Studies Program. The American Indian Studies curriculum and the AIS committee under the chairmanship of Dr. Dozier will serve to coordinate their varied contributions while in no way interfering with the autonomy of their particular disciplines" (EPD4.6, undated Ford Foundation proposal, 2–3).

The proposed AIS program would give priority to recruiting American Indian faculty members who were "uniquely capable of providing creative insights into their chosen fields and of attracting both Indian and non-Indian students to the interdisciplinary

Indian Studies Program" (EPD4.6, undated Ford Foundation proposal, 2). This proved to be an unattainable goal, because there were so few Native Americans with doctorates at the time who could meet the disciplinary qualifications for a faculty appointment. Even so, the new proposal insisted that this should be an area of faculty growth:

> *Faculty.* The most pressing need in strengthening our American Indian Studies Program at present is the addition of faculty members of American Indian descent. From among a growing number of young American Indian scholars the Committee on American Indian Studies has selected five scholars to invite to the University. These five individuals, representing five separate academic disciplines, are highly esteemed scholars. In addition to the scholars of American Indian descent, the Committee is seeking salary support for two outstanding linguists who have demonstrated their concern for American Indian education and have worked out a novel and effective method of teaching American Indian languages. (EPD4.6, undated Ford Foundation proposal, 6–7)

The proposed seven AIS faculty positions would consist of two full professorships, two associate professorships, and three assistant professorships. Salaries would range from $14,000 to $20,000 (EPD 4.1, Thompson to Carr, April 20, 1971). The departments that had already expressed interest in hiring American Indian faculty members and non-indigenous linguists included anthropology, art, English, history, and law. Longer-range placements would include architecture, economics, medicine, music, sociology, and philosophy (EPD4.6, undated Ford Foundation proposal, 2).

As the Committee on Indian Affairs worked on its revised proposal, its members continued to communicate with the Ford Foundation. Dozier traveled to New York City to consult with John Scanlon, a special projects staff member at the foundation, on "an informal version of the proposal" (EPD4.1, Thompson to UA comptroller Sherwood Carr, April 20, 1971). Scanlon explained that the scope of the program and the amount requested were beyond its allocation for ethnic studies. The foundation wanted to forge a financial partnership with UA rather than cover the program's full costs.

Eventually Ford offered to pay partial costs totaling $500,000 for seven faculty positions on an annually diminishing basis—80 percent the first year, decreasing to 20 percent the fifth year. The approved faculty hires would be two linguists and five native scholars in any discipline. The foundation expected the university to pay an increasing percentage of their salaries and bear the entire cost after the five-year grant period (EPD4.1, Scanlon to Thompson, March 25, 1971). Finally, it recommended that the committee revise and resubmit its grant proposal according to these terms, and the university complied. The committee (Dozier, Thompson, Fontana, Weaver, and Cecil Robinson) mailed its revised proposal to the Ford Foundation in the fall of 1970.

Sadly, Edward Dozier would not live to learn the results or to implement the program for which he had worked so hard. He had already suffered recent health problems. After a long delay in diagnosis, he had undergone surgery at Stanford Medical Center in April or May 1970 to remove a benign brain tumor and then suffered a stroke that left him with partial paralysis and dysphasia (Migué Dozier, personal communication, 2006). He had returned to teaching in the fall of 1970, but the spring semester of 1971 would be his last. On the evening of May 1 Dozier hosted a party at his home for Southwestern anthropologists who were in town for a conference. He died of a heart attack the following day. Just as he had warmly greeted his guests that evening, only days later his Pueblo relatives and friends would welcome him home to rest at Santa Clara Pueblo. He was fifty-five years old. His death, ending a twenty-year career, came at a time when Dozier stood at the threshold of a new opportunity to lead a major American Indian Studies program.

Two months after Dozier's death, in July 1971, the University of Arizona received a $500,000 grant from the Ford Foundation to launch its American Indian Studies program. In a report to the foundation, the administration praised Dozier for his role in AIS: "Dr. Dozier had established the philosophical basis for the program and had provided the leadership so necessary to the implementation of the program" (AIS office files, narrative report to Ford No. 71–371, Development of Graduate Program in American Indian Studies, ca. 1974).

Dozier's premature death raised the question of who would become chair of the new program. The university wanted an Indian scholar "who shared in the major features of Dr. Dozier's basic approach" (AIS office files, narrative report to Ford No. 71–371, Development of Graduate Program in American Indian Studies, ca. 1974). It chose Emory Sekaquaptewa, then assistant coordinator of Indian programs. He became director of American Indian Studies and assistant professor in the Department of Anthropology. In 1971 UA offered fifteen anthropology courses cross-listed under American Indian Studies. Among them were Clara Lee Tanner's "Native Peoples of the Southwest," "Ethnology of North America," and "Southwestern Indian Arts"; William Longacre's "Archaeology of the Southwest" and "Archaeology of North America"; Bernard Fontana's "History of the Indians of North America"; William Kelly's "Introduction to Applied Anthropology"; William Rathje's "Mesoamerican Archaeology"; Patrick Culbert's "Archaeology of South America"; and Keith Basso's "Ethnology of the Southwest."

As it turned out, most of the faculty members hired with the Ford Foundation money were non-Indian scholars with Indian research interests. The probability that there were few qualified Indian scholars at the time who could pass the rigorous hiring standards had been anticipated in the Ford grant proposal. In the end, three new professors joined the anthropology department in the early 1970s: Jerrold Levy, a medical anthropologist who studied the Navajos, and Susan Philips and Richard Diebold, both linguists with Native American language interests, although the latter was mainly an Indo-Europeanist.

Joyotpaul Chaudhur, an East Indian who had grown up on the

Choctaw reservation and married a Creek woman, was hired in the Department of Political Science and Government; he later directed the Asian Studies Program at Arizona State University in Tempe. In 1974 the English Department recruited Larry Evers, who had experience working on the Omaha reservation. Evers developed the Native American literary series "Sun Tracks," published by the University of Arizona Press. American Indian writers were invited to the university to give occasional presentations but were not offered faculty positions. E. Adamson Hoebel, a specialist in Indian law, became a visiting professor in anthropology and law (AIS office files, undated AIS program development proposal).

Only one Native American was hired under the Ford Foundation grant—Joseph (Jay) Stauss (Jamestown Band S'Kallam), a new Ph.D. in sociology from Washington State University with a research interest in urban Indians. After the five years funded by the Ford grant, the sociology department did not grant him tenure, although Stauss stayed on at UA in other capacities.

Despite these initial hires, the AIS program after Dozier's death emerged slowly. Over the next thirty years it gradually took on the shape Dozier had envisioned for it—an academic path for American Indian students in higher education. One setback was that not long after the Ford Foundation provided the seed money for the program, it reviewed the administration of its grant and withdrew its funding for the fifth year, 1975.

The loss of the Ford money led to significant internal factionalism at UA. One faculty member believed the foundation had considered the program incoherent, without a recognizable identity. The foundation thought the faculty it had funded were so scattered among diverse departments that they were nearly invisible. Later faculty members in the AIS program suggested the possibility of financial mismanagement by the Department of Anthropology, which coordinated the program and administered the funds. They additionally speculated that the Ford Foundation grant had been used not to build an American Indian Studies program but to further develop a four-field approach in anthropology by hiring more faculty to teach American Indian linguistics in a department already known for archaeology, ethnology, and physical anthropology.

When the department had hired Dozier himself in 1960, it had launched its permanent program in anthropological linguistics. He had taught courses such as "Introduction to Linguistics," "Language in Culture," and "American Indian Languages." His linguistic teaching duties were reduced after the arrival of two new anthropological linguists, Kenneth Hale and Keith H. Basso, and in 1969 he was released from linguistics instruction altogether. He then taught only cultural courses, such as "Social Structure and Organization," "Peoples of the Pacific," "Contemporary Southeast Asia," and an occasional seminar with Edward Spicer on the Greater Southwest.

Even with the hiring of Hale and Basso, the department by the mid-1960s had decided that its "linguistics offerings need to be strengthened by the improvement of facilities and opportunities.... The number and variety of Indian languages still spoken in Arizona and closely related areas are greater than for any other region of the country. The program in anthropological linguistics should be a vigorous one because of these important resources" (Annual Report, UA Department of Anthropology, 1965–66). To accomplish this, the department wanted to establish a Center for the Study of American Indian Languages. Although it never materialized, the plan for the center may have led to the hiring of Philips and Diebold with Ford Foundation funds, thus affecting the AIS program.

That the AIS program was originally administered through the Department of Anthropology in the College of Liberal Arts may have reflected a contemporary mindset in which the study of American Indians belonged most appropriately to the discipline of anthropology. By being expanded into a four-field department with additional strength in American Indian linguistics, anthropology would enhance its status and achieve higher standings in national rankings.

AIS faculty at the University of Arizona, however, felt that the

Ford grant did not institutionalize a new program of American Indian Studies but merely strengthened existing offerings on Indian topics by non-Indian faculty (UA, undated AIS program development proposal). In an interview, Vine Deloria Jr., a former chair of the AIS program, complained of empire building within the anthropology department: "It was obvious that [anthropology] ... was getting a whole bunch of white anthros and they were just teaching what courses they wanted and calling it Indian Studies" (Vine Deloria Jr., interview, July 10, 1990).

The economics and politics surrounding the Ford Foundation grant and the effort to build an autonomous American Indian Studies program at the University of Arizona were complex. The basic problem may have been lack of institutional support by UA, which failed to commit the promised funds to maintain the AIS program at the end of the initial Ford grant. Whatever the reason, AIS took a long and turbulent route to removing itself from the anthropology department and becoming established as an independent program at UA.

The 1970s saw repeated changes in funding, leadership, and programs. Led by a new chair, Joseph Stauss, the program was reorganized in 1976 toward American Indian leadership training. In 1978 the Ford Foundation, which had continued its commitment to Indian education (Henry 1972), awarded UA a grant to establish a master's degree program in Indian policy with an emphasis on leadership training. It was organized as a joint venture of the political science department and AIS and was directed by Vine Deloria Jr. Like the earlier award in 1971, the Ford grant stipulated that within the five-year grant period UA would make an institutional commitment to the program. Apparently it again failed to do so (AIS office files, American Indian Studies faculty 1991:46). But the AIS program persevered, and in 1982 UA approved it as a separate, interdisciplinary program headed by Robert K. Thomas (Cherokee). By the mid-1980s the university had begun offering AIS as a doctoral minor.

Ultimately, in 1997, with the program again under Stauss's direction, UA became one of the few universities in the United

States to offer a doctoral degree in an independent American Indian Studies program, which now had its own faculty and budget (Stauss, Fox, and Lowe 2002). Over time, its core faculty and student body became increasingly representative of diverse American Indian cultures.

Although the journey to full academic standing was slow, as the program matured it drew closer to Edward Dozier's original vision of American Indian education (Dozier 1969c). Overall, Dozier provided native leadership during the formative years of AIS. Although constrained by external foundation policies and insufficient administrative support, he helped put a leading Western university on a path toward restructuring higher education and incorporating indigenous needs, values, and scholarship into the academy.

8

From Paradox to Paradigm

For Edward P. Dozier, who has traveled these paths before us.
—Alfonso Ortiz, dedication in
New Perspectives on the Pueblos

At the outset of his career in the 1950s, Edward Dozier faced a dual paradox that was based upon his indigenous identity. That is, from the perspectives of both his own cultural community and the academy, he should not and could not, as an American Indian, become an anthropologist. Yet he did so. By conscientiously balancing the opposing values of a traditional community and the social sciences, he managed to construct a path that respected Pueblo traditional law regarding the secrecy of ritual knowledge and anthropological tenets regarding the objectivity of scientific research.

Over the course of twenty years, Edward Dozier created an original and complex career in anthropology that permitted him to study Pueblo Indian cultures and yet be accepted in both cultural and academic communities. Although he was a reticent and self-effacing person who did not promote himself to get ahead, he made substantial scholarly contributions as a native anthropologist. Keith H. Basso, a colleague of Dozier's at the University of Arizona, described him as "a fully engaged anthropologist" who was "unambitious professionally [yet] had a successful career in anthropology" (Keith H. Basso, interview, May 12, 1993).

Dozier was a pivotal figure in a historical continuum of American Indian scholars who contributed to public understanding of their indigenous languages and cultures. As a pioneer American

Indian anthropologist, he helped to improve the relationship between American Indians and universities, specifically in the ways in which Indians participated in field research and were represented in print. His career, from 1952 to 1971, exemplified a new era in terms of the roles of American Indians in the production of anthropological knowledge—roles that had changed from trail guide to interpreter, linguistic resource, data collector, field assistant, coauthor, and finally sole author.

Like a small number of American Indian scholars in museums and government positions before him, Dozier made advances in university life, forging his complex biological, cultural, and linguistic identities into professional strengths as an academic anthropologist. He belonged to a relatively inconspicuous first generation of American Indian scholars in the academy, along with D'Arcy McNickle at the University of Saskatchewan. A more conspicuous second generation followed Dozier and McNickle, in various disciplines. Its members included Alfonso Ortiz (San Juan Pueblo) at Princeton University and the University of New Mexico in anthropology, John Bodine (Taos Pueblo) at Marquette and American Universities in anthropology, N. Scott Momaday (Kiowa–Jemez Pueblo) at the Universities of Arizona and New Mexico in English, and Vine Deloria Jr. (Standing Rock Sioux) at the Universities of Arizona and Colorado in law, history, religious studies, and political science.

Although Dozier was constrained by the historical paradox of his time, he could claim several accomplishments. He demonstrated how scientific norms of objectivity could be interwoven with tribal perspectives in academic anthropology. His achievement of full professorial status made him a role model for future native students and faculty. His national reputation gave American Indian scholars a visible new legitimacy and authority in shaping academic and public policies. And his ethnography of the Kalingas in the Philippines effectively countered the stereotype that an American Indian anthropologist was qualified to study only his own people. Ultimately, Dozier exerted a subtle but significant influence on the development of American Indian scholars in the academy and on the emergence of American Indian Studies programs.

His many accomplishments were grounded in his method for resolving the dual paradox, at least partially, by respecting the truths on both sides, academic and tribal. Cultural truths are contextualized, and Dozier acknowledged the coexistence of multiple histories and cultural realities in his native anthropology. Another Santa Clara Pueblo scholar explained the multiple layers of cultural truths and understandings in this way:

> Truth is *not* absolute in the Pueblo world. There is never *one* truth. The world, the cosmos, the whole is multi-faceted and expresses many truths at once. Simultaneous levels of existence, as told in the Pueblo emergence stories, are a part of daily reality and understanding. Wholes (the cosmos, the community) are what must be experienced because parts (which can be wholes in their own context) give only a partial sense of understanding. There is, then, no set truth because contexts always change given any particular stance or reality. Because wholes are ever-changing, the effort to perceive wholes is unending—therefore, absolute truth is never attained. (Swentzell 1992:n.p.)

Edward Dozier was a modest man whose career was a quiet quest to explain the diversity and persistence of Pueblo Indian communities. He interpreted Pueblo behavior as both a kinsman and a social scientist. In his writings, for example, he represented Pueblo factionalism as an adaptive social and political process that might "help in the accommodation process" (Dozier 1970a:81–82). In his fieldwork he searched for patterns of the persistence of Pueblo cultures and sought pragmatic local interpretations of culture change. Writing about the Philippine Kalingas, he revealed how the adoption of legal arbitration and regional peace pacts had transformed headhunting in the twentieth century. Speaking to his academic colleagues, he questioned stereotypes of "primitive" people in the anthropological literature and recommended reforms in the value-laden words anthropologists used to describe modern-day indigenous people—many of whom were now literate, educated professionals like himself.

He was also an early advocate for indigenous rights. As a member of the American Anthropological Association's Ethics Committee, which drafted a formal statement on professional ethics in the mid-1960s, Dozier advocated for the minority rights of people in studied communities (Anita Alvarado, interview, December 5, 1990). In addition, he helped influence public policy at the national level through his participation as a member and later vice president of the Association on American Indian Affairs.

In his struggle to overcome the paradox of the American Indian anthropologist, Dozier revealed the critical importance of funding in the success of American Indian higher education. He benefited from a New Deal educational loan program under the Indian Reorganization Act in the mid-1930s, from the GI Bill after his military service in World War II, from a John Hay Whitney Opportunity Fellowship for minorities in the 1950s, from the Ford Foundation's educational policy initiatives for minority youths in the 1960s, and from other grants from private foundations and governmental agencies. The lack of economic support for American Indian higher education prior to the 1930s partially explains why it took so long for American Indians to become anthropologists.

Dozier has generally been overlooked in the history of American anthropology and American Indian Studies, partly because of his reserved Pueblo personality, which inclined him not to stand out from the group. His early efforts to recruit and hire American Indian faculty have been underrepresented in publications on AIS outside of the University of Arizona. He is either absent from the texts (Bilosi and Zimmerman 1997; Mihesuah 1998) or simply named in a list of Indian scholars (Bilosi 2004; Thornton 1998). Although he was a founding member of AIS at Arizona, Dozier is now remembered only faintly in its history or that of anthropology. Perhaps his quiet, conservative nature made him easy to forget, or perhaps his early death diminished his legacy—although Edward Sapir died at the same age but had a profound effect on anthropological linguistics (Darnell 1990). Dozier's characteristic self-effacement may have made him less noticeable than some later American Indian writers and scholars with greater public visibility and prestigious awards, such as Scott Momaday, who won the 1968 Pulitzer Prize in fiction for *House Made of Dawn*.

Dozier deserves more credit from the academy than he has received. He opened an academic path that enabled successive generations of American Indian students and faculty to study their own cultures. This achievement was unprecedented in the history of anthropology and in American higher education. Together with other, like-minded scholars and supporters, he helped transform academic studies of American Indians, once the exclusive domain of non-Indian anthropologists, into an intercultural and intertribal endeavor carried out by or in collaboration with American Indian students and faculty.

One of his most enduring contributions was institutional change—the emergence of a new structural relationship between the academy, anthropology, and American Indians. This quiet and symbolic revolution in academic politics partially, though not fully, transformed indigenous anthropology from a historical paradox into a contemporary paradigm. Along with the new infrastructure of American Indian Studies programs came a revolution of ideas and values that was reflected in the curriculum. With American Indian leadership, AIS provided a programmatic way for universities to incorporate indigenous systems of knowledge into Western curricula and, as a result, strengthen higher education.

The emergence of American Indian Studies programs on university campuses challenged the hegemony of anthropology over American Indian research from the third quarter of the twentieth century onward. The dialogue about indigenous issues diffused across academic disciplines—law, history, political science, agriculture, economics, education, literature, and medicine. By the twenty-first century, American Indian faculty had gained greater political power as tenured and tenure-track scholars who specialized in interdisciplinary and indigenous issues. They were no longer an anomaly but a paradigm of diverse native voices in universities.

As Dozier's career illustrates, the academic paradox of American Indians as anthropologists was not so much fully resolved in the discipline as it was redefined and renegotiated within the academy. Indeed, there has been no dramatic increase in the number of American Indian ethnographers since Dozier's death in 1971, although shortly afterward the American Anthropological Association produced a report titled "The Minority Experience in Anthropology" (Hsu et al. 1973) to encourage the recruitment and hiring of minorities. Instead, American Indian Studies has frequently been the path American Indians have taken as an alternative route to higher education, outside of anthropology. Like other ethnic studies programs, AIS was based upon a model of higher education that crossed boundaries among academic disciplines and combined them into new ways of learning.

Dozier's successful career in anthropology did not overcome the complex conflicts inherent in the indigenous paradox that culturally constrained an American Indian from becoming an anthropologist. One factor in Dozier's inability to resolve this aspect of the paradox was his academic writing and publishing. Whereas Pueblo Indian communities valued direct, experientially acquired personal knowledge, an anthropologist by definition gained knowledge of a culture through indirect means such as books. In the Pueblo knowledge system, a person could speak with authority only about what he or she had learned firsthand. Speaking for another person, as an anthropologist did, was unacceptable, because that knowledge belonged to the experience of someone else.

American Indian identity is a complex issue. Pueblo people can distinguish members of their community in various cultural and biological ways. A primary criterion is linguistic—one's ability to speak the local dialect well and knowledgeably. In this area, Dozier used the Tewa language informally in his social relations with Pueblo people and in his academic research with anthropological linguists throughout his life. One Pueblo person recalled meeting him and talking in their language:

I would see him every now and then, [and] of course, we would talk Tewa then together. I would ask him about his family and he would ask me about my family and so we conversed in Tewa.

Edward did like to talk in Tewa and I think he encouraged all his relatives to teach their children to speak in Tewa.

We went to visit Edward at his home [in Tucson]. And his home was just [like the] Pueblo style inside with vigas across and he had all his blankets so far on there. It was a very simple home, I thought. . . . And the first thing he asked . . . was, I guess in Tewa, "Have you been fed?" He wanted to know if we'd had our supper. Edward started talking in Tewa right away. (Pueblo interview, October 10, 1990)

But knowledge of the language alone is not enough. As another Pueblo person noted, "You can speak the language and still not have the slightest idea of what you're really saying" (Pueblo interview, December 7, 1990). That is, language competency was not always equivalent to cultural proficiency.

Because of his university career outside of New Mexico, Dozier was unable to reside at Santa Clara Pueblo. He spent his adult years away from the reservation, returning in the summers and holidays when his work allowed. His family had left the pueblo when he was twelve, and he attended schools far from the community thereafter. He apparently did not participate in ritual dances, ditch cleaning, or other community activities. No information is available about whether he was ever initiated, but it is probable that he lacked any substantial knowledge of Tewa religion and ceremonialism. As far back as his work with Elizabeth Sergeant on the Wild Flower Project in the mid-1930s, he recalled being scolded by an elder whom he had consulted about the native names and cultural meanings of native plants, because he had pulled up a flower that was considered sacred (EPD3.4, 3). He himself did not have that specialized knowledge.

Moreover, the Santa Clarans held deep suspicions of ethnographies of themselves, because earlier anthropologists had published information they considered privileged and proprietary. In 1929 the anthropologist Elsie Clews Parsons published *The Social Organization of the Tewa of New Mexico.* Later, during the 1940s, when W.W. Hill conducted ethnographic fieldwork at Santa Clara, he twice encountered people's extreme emotions about Parsons's book. One interviewee launched a verbal assault on Parsons's informant for breaking the long-standing customary law against telling village secrets to an outsider. The second incident was sparked by Hill's working with people who had earlier worked with other anthropologists. When Hill approached one of Parsons's informants, he wrote, "the man, since deceased, knew he was suspect, having previously been subjected to criticism. He informed the interpreter [Dozier] that no one ever gave such information; confronting him with Parsons' book almost resulted in a case of shock—the man turned pale, shook, and was unable to speak" (Hill 1982:143).

Sixty years later, Santa Clarans in 1990 perceived Hill's ethnography—which was edited, annotated, and published posthumously by Charles H. Lange—in much the same way they remembered Parsons's. They referred to Hill's volume as "*the* book" or "*that* book." One consultant explained: "I think a large percentage of the population have heard of that Santa Clara book. Yeah. They call it "*that*" Santa Clara book . . . and as soon as you hear "*that* Santa Clara book," you know it's Lange's book" (Pueblo interview, November 29, 1990). In Santa Clarans' eyes, "*the* book" exposed details about ceremonial life, and they denigrated it for its breach of Pueblo ethics. It included information and images that were secret and privileged, known only to a few select religious leaders in the pueblo. According to traditional law and customs, outsiders and uninitiated persons should not know these things.

Dozier's book *The Pueblo Indians of North America* was generally less well known among Santa Clarans than Hill's book in the late twentieth century. "There is an awareness that the [Hill] book is out there" one person said, and added:

> My impression is that very few people would know that book on the Rio Grande Pueblos. . . . There's a small percentage of them that would have taken the time to read the book. Those young college kids that are going to school now may use that as a resource book. People who are teachers . . . may make sure that is one of the reference books . . . because . . . it's a natural reference book if you're teaching a group of Indian students. (Pueblo interview, November 29, 1990)

Nevertheless, some Santa Clarans who did know of Dozier's publications but had never read them equated them with Hill's ethnography. Generally, anthropology books on the Pueblos were considered to be all the same; they were categorically dismissed and avoided. Sometimes people confused Hill's release of ritual knowledge with Dozier's books. In the larger moral picture, some Pueblo individuals believed it made no difference that Dozier generally avoided writing in any detail about Pueblo religion. He was a writer of books, and "books told secrets."

Evidence suggests that some Pueblo people considered an indigenous anthropologist such as Dozier an outsider despite his birthright and language skills. One Pueblo person felt that full membership as an insider involved much more than being born in a particular village:

> An insider in the professional world must abide by clearly delineated steps—he must follow the rules of objective research as prescribed. It can be tedious, but entry for anyone is possible. Achieving the role of insider in the Pueblo world at large is more limited—one must be Indian (Pueblo) (speak the language), and act as if one grew up in an Indian community. . . . You assumed that since Dozier was from St. Clara he was automatically an insider. That is not the case. If the Pueblo community feels that one of their own is writing about them, the pressures against them are tremendous. Dozier . . . was viewed by the inside community as an outsider. (Pueblo Indian letter, February 12, 1993)

At the same time, Dozier remained well liked and was always welcomed on his visits home to Santa Clara Pueblo, which he made as frequently as his university teaching commitments allowed. His relatives lived there, and he entrusted his daughter Wanda to the care of his brothers and sisters, who raised her at the pueblo. He maintained lifelong friendships there, as the attendance at his funeral attested. Although he led an academic life away from the village, he never crossed a boundary that made him resented or unwelcome in his native community.

Indeed, Dozier was invited several times in his younger years to consider serving as an officer on the Santa Clara Tribal Council. Because he was living away from the pueblo so much of the time, he felt he was unable to accept. As he explained during a meeting at Hopi in 1950: "I have been away from the pueblo so that I could not really serve practically. I was asked a number of times but I didn't because I knew I had to be away and an officer in the council should be in the pueblo as much as possible" (EPD4.1, Dozier, Hopi Tribal Council meeting at Kyakotsmovi [sic] Village, February 9, 1950). Several Santa Clarans recalled that in the 1960s the Santa Clara Tribal Council asked Dozier to testify on behalf of the pueblo at congressional hearings on the Indian Civil Rights Act. It appears, then, that by this criterion Dozier retained his community's respect, and his expertise as an anthropologist was considered useful to the pueblo's interests.

Nevertheless, anthropology remains generally suspect in Pueblo Indian communities today. After more than a century and a half of having been objects of scientific study, the Pueblos do not welcome purely academic research in their communities. Instead, the research must be relevant to current tribal needs and in accord with current cultural preservation initiatives, such as native language policies and land and water rights litigation. The work of anthropologists, including that of Edward Dozier, is critiqued from the changing perspectives of tribal policies. Over time, scholarly research on native cultures can be found wanting. For example, if current policy on language instruction allows a pueblo's language to be only spoken, not written, then the publications of earlier anthropological linguists, including Dozier, will be in disfavor.

Later generations of Pueblo Indians with college and postgraduate degrees in various disciplines are slowly easing some of the resistance to scholarly research. In the twentieth century, Santa Clara Pueblo produced three generations of scholars and other professionals, including artists, educators, historians, sociologists, anthropologists, museum professionals, physicians, business administrators, and librarians. These people made and continue to make direct and useful connections between their academic disciplines and the needs of their community. In addition, representatives on the Santa Clara Tribal Council have formed research partnerships with universities on matters of mutual interest. For example, the council is currently collaborating with the University of Pennsylvania Museum of Archaeology and Anthropology on a five-year oral history project (2005–10) to research a tribal history of the pueblo's 1935 constitution under the Indian Reorganization Act (Santa Clara Pueblo 1935). Together, a tribal government and a research university are showing how research partnerships can strengthen and serve both indigenous communities and the academy.

Such collaborations are part of Edward P. Dozier's legacy in American Indian higher education. He created an alternative path for native people in the academy, and his achievements will benefit future generations of American Indian scholars, who may, in their university and tribal communities, in some way experience the paradox of the American Indian anthropologist.

In retrospect, it is no wonder that Edward Pasqual Dozier's funeral in 1971 drew such a diversity of people—Pueblo Indians, white anthropologists, and Hispanic neighbors. He had spent his entire life and career interacting and communicating with people from differing backgrounds. This man called Awa see Tsire had traveled across cultural borders with humor, tolerance, patience, and respect. Through him we see the interconnectedness of humanity. He recognized all of us as his relatives.

Epilogue
Eulogy to Edward P. Dozier, by David Warren

David Warren is a historian, a friend of the Dozier family's, and a member of Santa Clara Pueblo; he was a colleague of Edward Dozier's. He gave the following eulogy at Dozier's funeral. The written version was an attachment to a letter from Warren to Marianne Dozier dated July 5, 1972 (EPD2.1). It is reproduced here with Warren's permission.

As a cycle is ended, a circle is closed. Edward has come home. It is appropriate that he should come home to rest in the land where life began, to the land he loved and to the place to which he brought honor in his life's travel. In the course of closing that circle his life touched many persons, in many places, throughout the world.

Scholars were proud to know him as a colleague and friend. Edward's work will be honored from this time forward. The contributions he made to the literature of human relations will enable others to forge further knowledge in the understanding of man. His place, although now empty, will be filled one day by another who was inspired by the life and works of Edward.

Indian people will remember him for the deep personal concern he had for their interests. Whether sitting in Pueblo council, or advocating for Indian interests at a national level, or setting the pace and theme in conferences on Indian education, Edward brought dignity and wisdom to the complex questions that face us in this age. His valued counsel and guidance will be missed. But he has inspired others among Indian youth to undertake the same course, in the same manner of deliberation. Indian education will be improved through the study and incorporation of the ideas he expressed, the words he spoke.

To his friends, the empty place he has left will remind us of what we took for granted: quiet patience, earnest counsel, understanding, loyalty. They will try to replace the empty place with others who must live by the standard set by Edward.

To his family, the loss is greatest and most private. Yet they are the fortunate ones. For in their daily lives, they knew him as father, husband, brother. They knew the depth and beauty of his love, a private privilege inaccessible to those who lived at the periphery of his life. Such love, while recalled with some sorrow, will sustain and strengthen.

In recent months, I have had occasion to search for answers to many questions that come from crisis. Again, at this time, these questions arise: at the time of being on the threshold of achieving goals and ideals he waited a lifetime for, Edward is suddenly taken; at the time when his insight and wisdom is badly needed by Indian people during a time of profound and confusing change, Edward is suddenly taken.

The answers are not clear nor perhaps ever are they really possible to know. But what has given me comfort is that we learn through these saddened moments to take stock of the precious lessons taught by men like Edward; we learn to value and seek out the friendships of men like him. But most of all, we try to reshape our lives according to what he left to us as part of our experience of growth and living.

Over 590 years ago, wise men, philosophers and religious poets gathered in the land now known as Mexico. They asked many of these same questions in the search for the true meaning of life and death. In their speeches, now left to us, they referred to the "flowers and the songs," symbols of poetry, beauty and truth. They said:

Will I have to go like flowers that perish?
Will nothing remain of my name?

Nothing of my fame here on earth?
At least my flowers, at least my songs!

These refrains remind us that Edward has left much for us. He will not perish. He has left much to be done; his inspiration and works will continue to guide the next steps in fulfilling many dreams. In his children he still lives and will continue in the character he moulded on their faces, in their hearts. He leaves strength to his wife in love and vivid remembrances of hard times, good times, their sharing. He will continue to guide all of us in the recollection of discussions of what he would have wanted us to do. Like the flowers and songs, Edward has left monuments and truth which are as enduring and broad as the valley of the Great River, as tall, strong and beautiful as Tsikomo.

We honor you, and we miss you, Edward.

Appendix A

Chronology of the Life of Edward P. Dozier

1916	Born April 23 to Thomas Sublette Dozier and Leocadia Gutierrez Dozier at Santa Clara Pueblo, New Mexico.
1923–26	Attends first through third grades at a Santa Fe County public school.
1925	Father, Thomas S. Dozier, dies May 24 at Thompson Ranch, Fairview, New Mexico.
1926–28	Attends fourth and fifth grades at Santa Clara Day School.
1928–29	Attends sixth grade at a public high school in Albuquerque.
1929–31	Attends seventh and eight grades at St. Michael's College, a predominately Hispanic Catholic boys' school in Santa Fe.
1931–35	Attends high school at St. Michael's College. Works during summers of 1933–35 as a laborer on Indian Emergency Conservation Work projects at Santa Clara Pueblo.
1935	Graduates from St. Michael's College. Works for federal government during summer as secretary and interpreter for Elizabeth Shepley Sergeant on Santa Clara Pueblo constitution and as assistant on Sergeant's Pueblo Wild Flower project. Enrolls in fall at University of New Mexico (UNM). Receives federal educational loan under Indian Reorganization Act (IRA) to attend college; boards at U.S. Indian School in Albuquerque.
1936	Votes in January in first election of tribal officers under new IRA constitution at Santa Clara Pueblo. Works as assistant during summer for Sergeant and as records clerk for employment bureau of United Pueblos Agency, Albuquerque.
1936–37	Works part-time 1936 and full-time 1937 as file clerk and typist for Emergency Conservation Work program of United Pueblos Agency. Projects include Pueblo Indian census.
1937	Leaves UNM in the fall. Takes job-hunting trip to Washington, DC, and New York City. Meets John Collier and J.P. Harrington; visits Elizabeth Shepley Sergeant.
1937–38	Works at U.S. Indian School, Albuquerque, as clerk and seventh-grade substitute teacher.

1938–39	Works as Indian assistant (mail and filing clerk) in construction division of Office of Indian Affairs, Washington, DC, November 1938–August 1939.
1939	Returns to college at UNM. Works as Indian assistant at U.S. Indian School, Albuquerque.
1940	Takes first course in anthropology at UNM.
1940–41	Participates as paid interpreter and facilitator on Santa Clara Pueblo ethnography with W.W. Hill, under sponsorship of National Youth Administration.
1941–45	Enlists in Army Air Force and serves four years of active duty. Basic training at Jefferson Barracks, Missouri. Assigned to intelligence school at Salt Lake City, Utah, to a B-17 crew in Chico, California, to a B-29 crew in Nebraska, and to the 873rd Squadron, 498th Bombardment Group, Saipan Island, Mariana Islands. Attains rank of staff sergeant.
1943	Marries Claire Elizabeth (Betty) Butler at St. Matthew's Catholic Church in Washington, DC, during a furlough in July.
1944	Daughter Wanda Marie born April 13 in Washington, DC.
1945	Conducts informal study of Chamorros in Charankanoa Village while stationed on Saipan. Returns to United States in October. Receives honorable discharge in California in November and returns to Santa Clara Pueblo.
1946	Works at Los Alamos National Laboratories, New Mexico. Separates from Betty Butler Dozier in August. Returns to UNM.
1947	Graduates from UNM in June with a BA in anthropology; begins graduate school in anthropology at UNM in September. Works on field research projects with anthropology department during summer.
1948	Is divorced from Betty Butler in May. Takes written master's examination at UNM during summer.
1948–49	Works as teaching assistant for Harry Hoijer at University of California–Los Angeles (UCLA).
1949	Graduates from UNM with MA in anthropology. Enrolls in new doctoral program in anthropology at UCLA; continues as Hoijer's teaching assistant. In June, takes written examination in ethnology. Conducts preliminary survey of Tewa Village on First Mesa, Hopi reservation. Receives predoctoral fellowship from Social Science Research Council.
1950	Mother, Leocadia Gutierrez Dozier, dies February 27 in U.S. Indian Hospital, Santa Fe. Dozier marries Marianne Fink in Flagstaff, Arizona, July 10. Takes Ph.D. qualifying examinations at UCLA in October.
1950–51	Conducts ethnographic fieldwork at Tewa Village (Hano) on

	Hopi reservation in Arizona with funding from a John Hay Whitney Foundation Opportunity Fellowship.
1951	Becomes member of Society of the Sigma Xi, UCLA chapter. Teaches a summer course on linguistics with Harry Hoijer at UC Berkeley. Defends doctoral dissertation at UCLA in December.
1951–52	Takes temporary position (sabbatical replacement) as lecturer in anthropology at University of Oregon, Eugene.
1952	*Newsweek* article "Dozier Dossier" appears March 24. Dozier graduates from UCLA in June with Ph.D. in anthropology and linguistics—first graduate of UCLA's doctoral program in anthropology and second American Indian to receive a doctorate in anthropology. Leads student ethnological field trip to Tewa Village in summer.
1952–53	Receives postdoctoral fellowship from Wenner-Gren Foundation for field study of cultural change among Southwestern Pueblos.
1953	Researcher, with Marianne Dozier, in July–August on segregation and integration in New Mexico and Arizona public schools, sponsored by Fund for the Advancement of Education, Ford Foundation.
1953–59	Teaches anthropology and linguistics at Northwestern University, Evanston, Illinois: instructor (1953–54), assistant professor (1954–57), associate professor (1958–59).
1954	Publishes monograph "The Hopi-Tewa of Arizona" (*University of California Publications in American Archaeology and Ethnology* 44[3]:259–376). Builds adobe house on three acres of land in Corrales, New Mexico.
1955	Elected first American Indian member of the board of directors, Association on American Indian Affairs, in May (serves until his death in 1971). Staff member on Southwestern Project in Comparative Psycholinguistics, sponsored by the Social Science Research Council, July–August. Son Migué born August 5 in Albuquerque.
1958–59	Fellow at Center for Advanced Studies in the Behavioral Sciences, Stanford University, Palo Alto, California. Makes field trip to Tewa Village with Stanford colleagues in April–May. Daughter Anya born March 29 in Palo Alto.
1959–60	Conducts ethnographic fieldwork with Kalinga people in northern Luzon, Philippines, with funding from a senior postdoctoral grant, National Science Foundation.
1960–71	Professor of anthropology and linguistics at the University of Arizona (UA), Tucson.
1961	Awarded a Penrose Fund grant to write book on Kalingas.

1961–62	Serves temporarily as American Indian student advisor at UA.
1963–64	Serves temporarily as chair of UA Committee on Indian Affairs.
1966	Publication of *Hano: A Tewa Indian Community in Arizona* (Holt, Rinehart and Winston) and of *Mountain Arbiters: The Changing Life of a Philippine Hill People* (University of Arizona Press). Spends sabbatical year in northern New Mexico studying Rio Grande Pueblo history and prehistory on Guggenheim fellowship.
1967	Publication of *The Kalinga of Northern Luzon, Philippines* (Holt, Rinehart and Winston).
1968	Elected chair of Indian Advisory Committee, UA. Elected second vice president of board of directors, Association on American Indian Affairs.
1969	Summer: Research grant from Rockefeller Foundation to Mindanao Island, Philippines. Works on planning First Convocation of American Indian Scholars at Princeton in March 1970 but is too ill to attend conference. Second term as fellow at Center for Advanced Studies, Stanford. October: Offered appointment by University of Minnesota as professor and chair of Department of American Indian Studies. Declines for health reasons.
1970	Publication of *The Pueblo Indians of North America* (Holt, Rinehart and Winston). Appointed chair of UA's new American Indian Studies Program (AIS). Submits grant proposals to foundations to fund AIS. Spring: undergoes surgery at Stanford Medical Center to remove a benign intracranial mass.
1971	Dies May 2 of a heart attack in Tucson, Arizona. Buried May 6 at Santa Clara Pueblo, New Mexico.

Appendix B
Edward P. Dozier: A Bibliography

This bibliography, with some additions and corrections, is based on one published by Fred Eggan and Keith H. Basso in their obituary for Edward Dozier in *American Anthropologist* (Eggan and Basso 1972).

Single-Authored Works

1948a	Review of *The Indians of the Americas,* by John Collier. *New Mexico Quarterly Review* 18:487–89.
1948b	Review of *Maria: The Potter of San Ildefonso,* by Alice Marriott. *Arizona Quarterly* 4:273–74.
1949	A Tentative Description and Classification of Tewa Verb Structure. Master's thesis, University of New Mexico, Albuquerque.
1951	Resistance to Acculturation and Assimilation in an Indian Pueblo. *American Anthropologist* 53(1): 56–66.
1952	The Changing Social Organization of the Hopi-Tewa. Ph.D. dissertation, University of California–Los Angeles.
1953	Tewa II: Verb Structure. *International Journal of American Linguistics* 19:118–27.
1954a	The Hopi-Tewa of Arizona. *University of California Publications in American Archaeology and Ethnology* 44(3): 259–376. Berkeley: University of California Press.
1954b	Spanish-Indian Acculturation in the Southwest: Comments. *American Anthropologist* 56(4): 680–84.
1954c	Review of *Kiva Mural Decorations at Awatovi and Kawaikaa-a, with a Survey of Other Wall Paintings in the Pueblo Southwest,* by Watson Smith. *American Anthropologist* 56(1): 141–42.
1955a	Kinship and Linguistic Change among the Arizona Tewa. *International Journal of American Linguistics* 21:242–57.
1955b	Forced and Permissive Acculturation. *American Indian* 7(2): 38–44.
1955c	The Concepts of "Primitive" and "Native." In *Yearbook of An-*

thropology, ed. William L. Thomas Jr., 187–202. New York: Wenner-Gren Foundation for Anthropological Research. Reprinted in *The Concept of the Primitive,* ed. Ashley Montagu, 229–56. New York: Free Press, 1968.

1955d Review of Papers from the Symposium on American Indian Linguistics held at the University of California–Berkeley, July 7, 1951. *American Anthropologist* 57:650–51.

1956a Two Examples of Linguistic Acculturation: The Yaqui of Sonora, Arizona, and Tewa of New Mexico. *Language* 32(1): 146–57. Reprinted in *Language and Culture,* ed. Dell Hymes, 509–20. New York: Harper and Row, 1965.

1956b The Values and Moral Concepts of the Rio Grande Pueblo Indians. In *Encyclopedia of Morals,* ed. Vergilius Ferm, 491–504. New York: Philosophical Library.

1956c The Role of the Hopi-Tewa Migration Legend in Reinforcing Cultural Patterns and Prescribing Social Behavior. *Journal of American Folklore* 69(272): 176–80.

1956d Review of *Navaho Acquisitive Values,* by Richard Hobson. *American Anthropologist* 58(4): 744–45.

1956e Review of *Third Annual Report of American Indian Development, 1954,* affiliated with the National Congress of American Indians. *American Anthropologist* 58(6): 1147–48.

1957a The Hopi and the Tewa. *Scientific American* 196:126–36. Reprinted in *Sociology: A Text with Adapted Readings,* eds. Leonard Broom and Philip Selznik, 75–78. Evanston, IL: Row Peterson, 1958. Reprinted in *Biology and Culture in Modern Perspective,* 313–17. San Francisco: W.H. Freeman, 1972. Reprinted in *New World Archaeology,* eds. Ezra B. Zubrow et al., 133–37. San Francisco: W.H. Freeman, 1974.

1957b Rio Grande Pueblo Ceremonial Pattern. *New Mexico Quarterly* 27(1): 27–34.

1957c Review of *An Ethno-Atlas: A Student's Manual of Tribal, Linguistic and Racial Groupings,* by Robert F. Spencer. *Journal of American Folklore* 70:289–90.

1957d Review of *Schoolcraft's Indian Legends,* edited by Mentor L. Williams. *Journal of American Folklore* 70:285–86.

1958a Ethnological Clues for the Sources of Rio Grande Population. In *Migrations in New World Culture History,* ed. Raymond H. Thompson, 21–32. University of Arizona Bulletin 29(2); Social Sciences Bulletin 27. Tucson: University of Arizona Press.

1958b Spanish-Catholic Influences on Rio Grande Pueblo Religion. *American Anthropologist* 60(3): 441–48.

1958c Cultural Matrix of Singing and Chanting in Tewa Pueblos. *International Journal of American Linguistics* 24(4): 268–72.

1958d   Review of *The Western Apache Clan System: Its Origin and Development*, by Charles R. Kaut. *Ethnohistory* 5:188–89.

1958e   Review of *Zuni Kin Terms*, by David M. Schneider and John M. Roberts, and *Zuni Daily Life*, by John M. Roberts. *American Anthropologist* 60(2): 385–86.

1960a   The Pueblos of the Southwestern United States. *Journal of the Royal Anthropological Institute* 90(1): 146–60. Reprint, Bobbs-Merrill Reprint Series A-374. Indianapolis: Bobbs-Merrill, 1966.

1960b   A Comparison of Eastern Keresan and Tewa Kinship Systems. In *Selected Papers of the Fifth International Congress of the Anthropological and Ethnological Sciences*, 96–186. Philadelphia: University of Pennsylvania Press.

1960c   A Comparison of Eastern Keresan and Tewa Kinship Systems. In *Proceedings of the Fifth International Congress of the Anthropological and Ethnological Sciences*, vol. 5, 430–36.

1961a   Rio Grande Pueblos. In *Perspectives in American Indian Culture Change*, ed. Edward H. Spicer, 94–186. Chicago: University of Chicago Press.

1961b   Land Utilization and Social Organization among the Pagan Peoples of Northern Luzon, Philippines. In *Papers Delivered at the Annual Meeting of the American Ethnological Society, Columbus, Ohio*, 2-6. Seattle: University of Washington Press.

1961c   Review of *Cochiti: A New Mexico Pueblo, Past and Present*, by Charles H. Lange. *Journal of American Folklore* 74:171–72.

1962a   The Kalinga of Northern Luzon, Philippine Islands. In *Yearbook, 1962*, 515–17. Philadelphia: American Philosophical Society.

1962b   Phonological Characteristics of Southwestern Indian Languages. In *Annual Conference of the Co-ordination Council for Research in Indian Education*. Phoenix: Arizona State Department of Public Instruction, Division of Indian Education.

1962c   Who Are the Parents of Children in Arizona? In *Report of a Conference for Nurses Working with Children, August 20–24, 1962*, 1–4. Tucson: University of Arizona School of Nursing.

1962d   Review of *Ceremonial Costumes of the Pueblo Indians*, by Virginia M. Roediger. *Journal of American Folklore* 75(296): 165–66.

1962e   Review of *Cochiti: A New Mexico Pueblo, Past and Present*, by Charles H. Lange. *Man* 183–85:109.

1962f   Review of *Fruitland, New Mexico: A Navaho Community in Transition*, by Tom Sasaki. *Man* 62:110.

1963a   Differing Reactions to Religious Contacts among North American Indian Societies. German translation. In *Proceedings of the Thirty-fourth International Congress of Americanists, Vienna, 18–25 July 1960*, 161–171. Horn: Verlag Ferdinand Berger.

1963b   Linguistics Pioneers in Southwestern Anthropology: A Symposium. *Journal of the Arizona Academy of Sciences* 2(3): 133–34.

1963c   The Linguist's Approach to Language with Implications for Language Teaching and Learning. In *Proceedings of the Second Annual Conference in Reading.* Tucson: Reading Development Center, University of Arizona.

1963d   Review of *On the Gleaming Way: Navajos, Eastern Pueblos, Zunis, Hopis, Apaches, and Their Land,* by John Collier. *American Anthropologist* 65(2): 441–42.

1963e   Review of *Isleta Paintings,* edited by E.S. Goldfrank. *American Anthropologist* 65(4): 936–37.

1964a   Some Thoughts about the "Psychological Reality" of Linguistic Units. In *On Teaching English to Speakers of Other Languages,* ed. Virginia French Allen, n.p. National Council of Teachers of English.

1964b   A Brief Description of Southwestern Indian Speech Sounds. In *Education of the American Indian in Today's World,* eds. Norman C. Greenberg and Gilda M. Greenberg, n.p. Dubuque, IA: W.M.C. Brown Book Company.

1964c   The Pueblo Indians of the Southwest. *Current Anthropology* 5(2): 79–97.

1964d   The Kalinga Peacepact Institution. In *Proceedings of the Sixth International Congress of Anthropological and Ethnological Sciences, Paris, 1960,* vol. 2, 315–19.

1964e   Review of *The Book of the Hopi,* by Frank Waters. *Arizona Quarterly* 20(1): 87–88.

1965a   Resistance to Acculturation and Assimilation. *American Anthropologist* 53:56–65.

1965b   Southwestern Social Units and Archaeology. *American Antiquity* 31(1): 38–47.

1965c   Review of *A Reconstruction of the Basic Jemez Pattern of Social Organization, with Comparisons to Other Tanoan Social Structures,* by Florence Hawley Ellis. *American Anthropologist* 67:802–3.

1965d   Review of *Pueblo Gods and Myths,* by Hamilton A. Tyler. *Journal of American Folklore* 78(307): 73–74.

1966a   *Hano: A Tewa Indian Community in Arizona.* Case Studies in Cultural Anthropology. New York: Holt, Rinehart and Winston.

1966b   *Mountain Arbiters: The Changing Life of a Philippine Hill People.* Tucson: University of Arizona Press.

1966c   Factionalism at Santa Clara Pueblo. *Ethnology* 15(2): 172–85.

1966d   Anthropology. In *Science Year,* the *World Book* science annual, 255–56.

1966e   Linguistic Acculturation in the Southwestern United States. In *Proceedings of the Thirty-sixth International Congress of Americanists, Seville,* vol. 2, 253–60.

1966f   Problem Drinking among American Indians: The Role of Sociocultural Deprivation. *Quarterly Journal of Studies on Alcohol* 27(1): 72–87.

1966g   Review of *Friends of Thunder: Folktales of the Oklahoma Cherokee*, by Anna G. Kilpatrick and Jack F. Kilpatrick. *Journal of American Folklore* 79(313): 483–84.

1966h   Review of *Life in a Leyte Village*, by Ethel Nurge. *Science* 151(3714): 1071–72.

1967a   *The Kalinga of Northern Luzon, Philippines.* Case Studies in Anthropology. New York: Holt, Rinehart and Winston.

1967b   Linguistic Acculturation Studies in the Southwest. In *Studies in Southwestern Ethnolinguistics*, eds. Dell H. Hymes and William E. Bittle, 389–402. The Hague: Mouton.

1967c   Review of *The Population of Borneo*, by L.W. Jones. *Science* 157(3792): 1028.

1967d   Review of *Divisiveness and Social Conflict: An Anthropological Approach*, by Alan R. Beals and Bernard J. Siegel. *Social Forces* 46(1): 118.

1968a   The Pueblos. Paper presented at the annual meeting of the American Association for the Advancement of Science, Dallas, 28 December.

1968b   Los indios pueblo de Arizona y Nuevo Mexico. *Anuario Indigenista* 28:191–97.

1968c   Range of Cultural and Linguistic Variation among American Indians. Paper presented at the Conference on Teaching of English as a Second Language, Stanford, CA, July 9.

1968d   Review of *On the Cordillera: A Look at the Peoples and Cultures of the Mountain Province*, by William Henry Scott. *American Anthropologist* 70(2): 383–84.

1968e   Understanding Indian Culture. *Youth* 19(17): 40–49.

1969a   Autogobierno y los pueblos del suroeste de los Estados Unidos. *Anuario Indigenista* 39:65–72.

1969b   Peasant Culture and Urbanization: Mexican Americans in the Southwest. In *Peasants in the Modern World*, ed. Philip K. Bock, 140–58. Albuquerque: University of New Mexico Press.

1969c   The Teacher and the Indian Student. *Indian History* 2(1): 9–11.

1970a   *The Pueblo Indians of North America.* Case Studies in Cultural Anthropology. New York: Holt, Rinehart and Winston. Reprint, Prospect Heights, IL: Waveland Press, 1983.

1970b   Making Inferences from the Present to the Past. In *Reconstructing Prehistoric Pueblo Societies*, ed. William A. Longacre, 202–13. Albuquerque: University of New Mexico Press.

1970c   Southwestern (USA) Pueblo Ethnology and Social Anthropology. *Proceedings of the International Congress of Anthropological and Ethnological Sciences, 1964, Moscow*, vol. 10, 429–34.

1970d	Theoretical and Methodological Contributions of Southwestern Anthropology. *Proceedings of the International Congress of Anthropological and Ethnological Sciences, 1964, Moscow,* vol. 11, 97–101.
1971a	The American Southwest. In *North American Indians in Historical Perspective,* eds. Eleanor B. Leacock and Nancy O. Lurie, 228–56. New York: Random House.
1971b	Review of *Languages and Cultures of Western North America: Essays in Honor of Sven S. Liljeblad,* edited by Earl H. Swanson Jr. *American Anthropologist* 73(6): 1376–77.
1972	Pueblo Indian Response to Culture Contact. In *Studies in Linguistics in Honor of George L. Trager,* ed. M. Estellie Smith, 457–67. The Hague: Mouton.
1984	Problem Drinking among American Indians: The Role of Sociocultural Deprivation. In *Mini Waka and the Sioux,* eds. Rodger Hornby and Richard H. Dana, 29–42. Brandon, Manitoba, Canada: Justin.

Coauthored Works

Hoijer, Harry, and Edward P. Dozier
1949	The Phonemes of Tewa, Santa Clara Dialect. *International Journal of American Linguistics* 15(3): 139–44.
Simpson, George F., J. Milton Yinger, and Edward P. Dozier
1957	The Integration of Americans of Indian Descent. *Annals of the American Academy of Political and Social Sciences* 31:158–65.

Appendix C
Edward P. Dozier Papers at the Arizona State Museum

The Edward P. Dozier Papers is a manuscript collection (number 23) in the Arizona State Museum Archives at the University of Arizona, Tucson, that I used extensively in my research. For this book, papers in the collection are cited using the abbreviation EPD, followed by the numbers of the subgroup and series—for example, "EPD1.1" for Subgroup 1, Series 1. For a more complete finding aid, refer to Appendix C in Norcini 1995.

Subgroup 1. Thomas Sublette Dozier papers, 1885–1919

Series 1. Correspondence
Series 2. Business records
Series 3. Family history
Series 4. Manuscripts
Series 5. Printed materials
Series 6. Account books and journals
Series 7. Business letter books

Subgroup 2. Edward P. Dozier personal papers, 1923–1970

Series 1. Biographical materials
Series 2. Family correspondence
Series 3. Diaries
Series 4. School records
Series 5. Financial records
Series 6. Military records
Series 7. Memorabilia
Series 8. Miscellaneous correspondence
Series 9. Miscellaneous journals, memo books, account books, and souvenirs

Subgroup 3. Elizabeth Shepley Sergeant papers, 1923–1964

Series 1. Correspondence
Series 2. Manuscripts, reports, and surveys
Series 3. Literary manuscripts, articles, book reviews
Series 4. Pueblo Wildflower book

Subgroup 4. Edward P. Dozier professional papers, 1935–1972

Series 1. Correspondence
Series 2. Hopi-Tewa (Hano)
Series 3. Kalinga ethnography
Series 4. Manuscripts
Series 5. Professional organizations and programs
Series 6. University records

Appendix D

Prenuptial Agreement between Thomas S. Dozier and Maria Leocadia Gutierrez, September 25, 1896

This document is preserved in the Edward P. Dozier Papers at the Arizona State Museum Archives, in Subgroup 1, Thomas Sublette Dozier papers, 1885–1919, Series 3, Family history.

English Transcription

This Agreement and Ante-Nuptial Contract made and entered into this Twenty fifth day of September, year of 1896, by and between Thomas S. Dozier, of the County of Santa Fé and Territory of New Mexico, and Maria Leocadia Gutierrez, of the County of Santa Fé and Territory of New Mexico;

Witnesseth: —

I. That the parties hereunto agreeing and signing these presents agree to be married within Sixty days from the date of this contract in accordance with the rites and ceremonies of the Roman Catholic Church.

II. The said Thomas S. Dozier agrees to maintain and keep the said Maria Leocadia Gutierrez as his lawful wife in every respect as if she were of his own race; to provide within the boundary lines of the Reservation of the Pueblo of Santa Clara a suitable home; to make and provide the proper means for the exercise of her religious belief and customs by reason of her being a member of the Roman Catholic Church and a member of the Pueblo of Santa Clara; he further agrees not to remove nor influence the said Maria Leocadia Gutierrez to remove from the said Reservation by any means whatsoever against her will or that of her now legal guardians at any time after the consummation of this contract, nor to induce her to change any customs, rules, rites or ceremonies which she or her now legal guardians may hold as binding by reason of her religious belief and previous training: provided such customs, rules, rites and ceremonies be not against morality; he further agrees that, under the favor of God, should children be born as a result of this marriage that he will not seek to have them taught a different religious belief from that of the party of the second part, and moreover that he will provide that there may be given by competent persons religious and Catholic instruction sufficient to enable them to make their first communions, the party of the first part only reserving the right of providing for their secular education; he further agrees that all lands or tenements now belonging to her or that may hereafter descend to her and all real estate that in the future may be purchased, any part of which three classes may lie within the boundary lines of the said Reservation shall be and continue to be recorded in the name of the said Maria Leocadia Gutierrez and shall pertain to her in her own right.

III. The said Maria Leocadia Gutierrez agrees to be a faithful wife to the said Thomas Sublette Dozier and conduct herself in every respect as duty and the rules of her religious belief enjoin; she moreover agrees not to influence nor induce others to influence, by any means whatsoever, the said Thomas Sublette Dozier to change any rules, customs, rites or ceremonies now pertaining to him or practiced by him by reason of his religious belief or previous training: provided, such rules, customs, rites and ceremonies be not against morality; she further agrees that all lands and tenements now pertaining to him or that may hereafter descend to him or that in the future may be purchased and not within the limits of the said Reservation shall be governed by the laws of descent of the place wherein the same may now or hereafter be situated.

IV. It is agreed by both parties to this contract that all other property of whatsoever nature shall be governed by the laws of the Territory of New Mexico and by the ancient customs and rules of the said Pueblo of Santa Clara.

V. The agreements above enumerated severally are hereunto agreed to by both the parties to this contract.

Witnesses:

Cosme Herrera   Tomas Sublette Dozier. (Seal)
For the party of the first part   Party of the first part.

Maria Lucia Herrera
Apolonio Vigil   Maria Leocadia Gutierrez. (Seal)
For the party of the second part Party of the second part.

Spanish Transcription

Este convenio y Contrato Ante-Nupcial hecho y convenido este dia vientecinco de Septiembre, Año de 1896, por y entre Tomas Sublette Dozier del Condado de Santa Fé y Territorio de Nuevo Mejico, y Maria Leocadia Gutierrez, del Condad de Santa Fé de Territorio de Nuevo Mejico;

Da Fé: —

I. Que las partes á este conviniendo y firmando estas presentes convienen contraer matrimonio dentro de sesenta dias desde la fecha de este contrato en conformidad con los ritos y ceremonias de la Iglesia Catolica Romana.

II. El dicho Tomas Sublette Dozier conviene en mantener y cuidar á la dicha Maria Leocadia Gutierrez como su legitima esposa en todo respecto, como si ella fuese de su propio prole; de proveer dentro de los linderos de la Reservacion del Pueblo de Santa Clara un hogar conveniente; de hacer y proveer los medios propios para el ejercicio de su creencia religiosa y costumbres, debido á ser ella un miembro de la Iglesia Catolica Romana, y miembro del Pueblo de Santa Clara; el ademas conviene no remover ni influir á la dicha Maria Leocadia Gutierrez de cambiarse de dicha Reservacion, por medios cualesquiera que sean, encontra de su voluntad, o la de sus presentes guardianes legales, en cualquier tiempo despues de la consumacion de este contrato, ni inducirla que ca[m]bie cualesquiera costumbres, ritos, reglas o ceremonias las cuales ella o sus guardianes legales puedan tener por obligacion por motivo de sus creencias religiosas y crianza previa: *proveido,* tales costumbres, relas, ritos y ceremonias no sean en contra de la moral; el ademas conviene que si por el favor de Dios naciesen hijos como resultado de su enlace, que él no ententará que se les enseñe una creencia religiosa diferente á la de la parte de la segunda parte, y ademas proverrá que les sea dado por personas competentes una instrucion religiosa y Catolica suficiente para que hagan sus primeras comuniones; la parte de la primera parte solamente reservando el derecho de proveer por su educacion seglar; el ademas conviene que todas las tierras o tenencias pertenecientes á ella ahora, o que en adelante puedan descender á ella por herencia, y toda la propiedad raiz que en lo futuro comprare, cualquiera parte de las cuales tres clases entren dentro de las lineas divisorias de la dicha Reservacion, serán y continuarán siendo registradas en el nombre de la dicha Maria Leocadia Gutierrez y pertenecerá á ella en su propio derecho.

III. La dicha Maria Leocadia Gutierrez conviene ser una fiel esposa al dicho Tomas Sublette Dozier, y conducirse así misma en todo respecto como el deber y reglas de su creencia religiosa ordenan; ademas ella conviene en no influir ni inducir á otros que influyan, por medios cualesquiera que sean, al dicho Tomas Sublette Dozier de cambiar cualesquiera reglas, costumbres, ritos o ceremonias ahora perteneciendole o practicadas por él, como parte de su creencia religiosa o crianza previa: *proveido,* tales reglas, costumbres, ritos y ceremonias no son en contra la moral; ella ademas conviene que todas las tierras y tenencias ahora pertenecientes á él, or pertenecerle á él pro herencia, o que en lo futuro comprare y que no esten dentro de los limites de dicha Reservacion serán gobernadas por las leyes de herencia del lugar donde las mismas estan o en adelante esten situadas.

IV. Es convenido por ambas partes á este contrato que todo otro propiedad de cualquiera naturaleza que sea, será gobernada por las leyes del Territorio de Nuevo Mejico y por costumbres antiguas y reglas del dicho Pueblo de Santa Clara.

V. Los convenios arriba enumerados separadamente son por este convenidos por ambas partes á este contrato.

Testigos:

Cosme Herrera (signed)   Tomas Sublette Dozier (Seal)
Por la parte de la primera parte.   Parte de la primera parte.

Maria Lucia Herrera (signed)
Apolonia Vigil (signed)   Maria Leocadia Gutierrez (Seal)
Por la parte de la segunda parte.   Parte de la segunda parte.

A true copy furnished Mrs. C.S. Hill for her information.

References

Abbreviations Used in References

EPD   Edward P. Dozier Papers. Refer to appendix C for numbers of subgroups and series given in the citations.
NAB   National Archives Building, Washington, DC
NARA   National Archives and Records Administration
NPA   Northern Pueblo Agency
RG 75   Record Group 75, Records of the Bureau of Indian Affairs
RM   Rocky Mountain Repository of NARA, Denver, Colorado

Archival and Manuscript Collections

Association on American Indian Affairs Archives, 1851–1995
 Formerly the Eastern Association on Indian Affairs. Seeley G. Mudd Manuscript Library, Manuscript Collection 147, Princeton University Library, Princeton, New Jersey.

Dozier, Edward P. Papers
 Arizona State Museum Archives, Manuscript Collection 23, University of Arizona, Tucson. Refer to appendix C.

Dozier, Edward P. Photographs
 Kalinga photographs by Edward P. Dozier. Arizona State Museum Photographic Archives, University of Arizona, Tucson.

Dozier, Thomas Sublette. Papers
 Arizona State Museum Archives, Manuscript Collection 23, Subgroup 1, University of Arizona, Tucson. Refer to appendix C.

Dozier Family Ledger Book and Family Bible
 In the possession of the Dozier family at Santa Clara Pueblo.

Dozier Family Records
 Correspondence and photographs in the possession of Edward Dozier's family at Santa Clara Pueblo, New Mexico.

Harrington, John Peabody. Papers
 National Anthropological Archives, National Museum of Natural History, Smithsonian Institution, Suitland, Maryland.

Hill, W.W. Papers
  Santa Clara Pueblo ethnographic field notes and a copy of Jean Allard Jeançon's Santa Clara Pueblo manuscript. Paper Archives, Maxwell Museum of Anthropology, University of New Mexico, Albuquerque.
National Archives and Records Administration
  Civil Service records, Bureau of Indian Affairs (BIA), Record Group 75. National Archives Building, Washington, DC.
National Archives and Records Administration
  National Personnel Records Center, St. Louis, Missouri.
National Archives and Records Administration
  Office of Indian Affairs records (BIA), Record Group 75, Rocky Mountain Region, Denver, Colorado, and National Archives Building, Washington, DC.
Sergeant, Elizabeth Shepley. Papers
  Yale Collection of American Literature, Manuscript 3, Beinecke Rare Book and Manuscript Library, Yale University, New Haven, Connecticut. Sergeant's archives on American Indian affairs were removed from this collection and interfiled with the John Collier Papers at Manuscripts and Archives, Sterling Library, Yale University. Other literary materials are in the Elizabeth Shepley Sergeant Papers, Manuscript 10, Special Collections Department, Bryn Mawr College Library. The Sergeant-Dozier correspondence and the Pueblo Wild Flower Project file are in the Edward P. Dozier Papers, Subgroup 3. Refer to appendix C.
Spicer, Edward H., and Rosamond B. Papers, 1911–2000
  Arizona State Museum Archives, Manuscript 5, University of Arizona, Tucson.
University of Arizona
  Edward P. Dozier's employee files in the Department of Anthropology and Library Special Collections, University of Arizona, Tucson.

Published Works

American Indian Studies faculty
1991   Academic Program Review: Self-Study. Tucson: American Indian Studies Research Center, University of Arizona.

Barton, Roy Franklin
1949   *The Kalingas: Their Institutions and Custom Law.* Chicago: University of Chicago Press.

Benedict, Ruth
1931   *Tales of the Cochiti Indians.* Bulletin of the Bureau of American Ethnology 98. Washington DC: U.S. Government Printing Office. Reprint, Albuquerque: University of New Mexico Press, 1981.
1934   *Patterns of Culture.* Boston: Houghton Mifflin.

Bilosi, Thomas, ed.
2004   *A Companion to the Anthropology of American Indians.* Malden, MA: Blackwell.

Bilosi, Thomas, and Larry J. Zimmerman, eds.
1997   *Indians and Anthropologists: Vine Deloria, Jr., and the Critique of Anthropology.* Tucson: University of Arizona Press.

Boas, Franz, and Ella Deloria
1941   *Dakota Grammar.* National Academy of Sciences Memoirs, vol. 23, no. 2. Washington, DC: U.S. Government Printing Office.

Boas, Franz, and George Hunt
1905–6 *Kwakiutl Texts.* Memoirs of the American Museum of Natural History, vol. 5. Leiden: E.J. Brill. Reprint, New York: AMS Press, 1975.

Bock, Philip K.
1989   Anthropology at the University of New Mexico, 1928–1988: A Trial Formulation. *Journal of Anthropological Research* 45(1): 1–14.

Bodine, John
1972   Acculturation Processes and Population Dynamics. In *New Perspectives on the Pueblos,* ed. Alfonso Ortiz, 257–85. Albuquerque: University of New Mexico Press.

Brandt, Elizabeth A.
1980   On Secrecy and the Control of Knowledge: Taos Pueblo. In *Secrecy: A Cross-Cultural Perspective,* ed. Stanton K. Tefft, 123–46. New York: Human Sciences Press.
1985   Internal Stratification in Pueblo Communities. Paper presented at the annual meeting of the American Anthropological Association, Washington, DC.

Bright, William
1964   Harry Hoijer's Writings through 1963. *International Journal of American Linguistics* 30:169–74.

Cajete, Gregory
1994   *Look to the Mountain: An Ecology of Indigenous Education.* Durango, CO: Kivakí Press.

Champagne, Duane, and Jay Stauss, eds.
2002   *Native American Studies in Higher Education: Models for Collaboration between Universities and Indigenous Nations.* Walnut Creek, CA: Altamira Press.

Champagne, Duane, Karen Jo Torjesen, and Susan Steiner, eds.
2005   *Indigenous Peoples and the Modern State.* Walnut Creek, CA: Altamira Press.

Cohen, Felix S.
1941   *Handbook of Federal Indian Law.* Washington, DC: U.S. Government Printing Office.

Culin, Stewart
1907	*Games of the North American Indians.* Twenty-fourth Annual Report of the Bureau of American Ethnology, 1902–3. Washington, DC: U.S. Government Printing Office.

Darnell, Regna
1990	*Edward Sapir: Linguist, Anthropologist, Humanist.* Berkeley: University of California Press.

Dauber, Kenneth
1990	Pueblo Pottery and the Politics of Regional Identity. *Journal of the Southwest* 32(4): 576–96.

Deloria, Ella
1932	*Dakota Texts.* Publications of the American Ethnological Society, vol. 14. New York: G.E. Stechert.

Deloria, Vine Jr., and Clifford M. Lytle
1969	*Custer Died for Your Sins: An Indian Manifesto.* New York: Macmillan.
1984	*American Indians, American Justice.* Austin: University of Texas Press.

Dozier, Edward P.
	Refer to appendix B for a comprehensive bibliography.

Dozier, Thomas Sublette (pseudonym Thomas S.D. Brumfield)
1894	The Teguas. *Cameron Sun* (Missouri). Part 1, March 9, 1894; Part 2, March 16, 1894; Part 3, March 23, 1894.
1921	Historical Pageantry at Santa Clara Pueblo. *El Palacio* (Museum of New Mexico) 10:98–99.

Eggan, Fred
1954	Notes and Comments: The Philippine Studies Program. *University of Manila Journal of East Asiatic Studies* 3(3): 325–27.
1955	Review of *The Hopi-Tewa of Arizona*, by Edward P. Dozier. *Ethnohistory* 2(3): 277–79.

Eggan, Fred, and Keith Basso
1972	Obituary for Edward P. Dozier. *American Anthropologist* 74(3): 740–46.

Fathauer, George H.
1955	Review of *The Hopi-Tewa of Arizona*, by Edward P. Dozier. *American Anthropologist* 57(6): 1305–6.

Feldman, Kerry D.
1981	Anthropology under Contract: Two Examples from Alaska. In *Anthropologists at Home in North America: Methods and Issues in the Study of One's Own Society,* ed. Donald A. Messerschmidt, 223–38. Cambridge: Cambridge University Press.

Fewkes, Jesse W.
1894	The Kinship of a Tanoan Speaking Community in Tusayan. *American Anthropologist,* old series, 7(2): 162–67.

Gallie, W. B.
1968 *Philosophy and the Historical Understanding.* New York: Schocken Books.

Getches, David H., Charles F. Wilkinson, and Robert A. Williams Jr.
1993 *Federal Indian Law: Cases and Materials.* American Casebook Series. St. Paul, MN: West Publishing.

Gupta, Akhil, and James Ferguson
1997 Culture, Power, Place: Ethnography at the End of an Era. In *Culture, Power, Place: Explorations in Critical Anthropology*, edited by Akhil Gupta and James Ferguson, 1–29. Durham, NC: Duke University Press.

Harrington, John P.
1910 *A Brief Description of the Tewa Language.* Papers of the School of American Archaeology (Archaeological Institute of America), no. 17. Reprint, *American Anthropologist* 12(4): 497–504.
1916 *The Ethnogeography of the Tewa Indians.* Annual Report of the Bureau of American Ethnology, 1907–8. Washington, DC: U.S. Government Printing Office.

Henry, Jeannette, ed.
1972 *American Indian Reader: Education,* vol. 2. San Francisco: Indian Historian Press.

Hill, W. W.
1982 *An Ethnography of Santa Clara Pueblo, New Mexico.* Edited and annotated by Charles H. Lange. Albuquerque: University of New Mexico Press.

Hinsley, Curtis M.
1981 *The Smithsonian and the American Indian: Making a Moral Anthropology in Victorian America.* Washington, DC: Smithsonian Institution Press.

Hoijer, Harry, and Edward P. Dozier
1949 The Phonemes of Tewa, Santa Clara Dialect. *International Journal of American Linguistics* 15:139–44.

Hopi Tribe of Arizona
1936 Constitution and Bylaws of the Hopi Tribe of Arizona. Approved December 19, 1936.

Hsu, Francis L. K.
1964 Rethinking the Concept "Primitive." *Current Anthropology* 5(3): 169–78.

Hsu, Francis L. K., Delmos Jones, Diane Lewis, Beatrice Medicine, James L. Gibbs, and Thomas Weaver
1973 *The Minority Experience in Anthropology: Report of the Committee on Minorities and Anthropology, August 1973.* Washington, DC: American Anthropological Association.

Jeançon, Jean Allard
1931   Santa Clara: A New Mexico Tewa Pueblo. Unpublished manuscript in W.W. Hill papers, Maxwell Museum of Anthropology, Paper Archives, University of New Mexico. 83 pages.

Jones, Delmos
1970   Towards a Native Anthropology. *Human Organization* 29(4): 251–59.

Jones, William
1901   Episodes in the Culture-Hero Myth of the Sauks and Foxes. *Journal of American Folk-Lore* 14:225–39.
1904   *Some Principles of Algonkin Word-Formation.* American Anthropologist, n.s., vol. 6, no. 3, supplement.
1905   The Algonkin Manitou. *Journal of American Folklore* 18 (70): 183–90.
1907   *Fox Texts.* Publications of the American Ethnological Society, vol. 1. Leyden: E.J. Brill.

Kahn, E.J. Jr.
1981   *Jock: The Life and Times of John Hay Whitney.* Garden City, NJ: Doubleday.

Kaut, Charles
1967   Review of *Mountain Arbiters: The Changing Life of a Philippine Hill People,* by Edward P. Dozier. *Science* 156(3783): 1722–23.

Kroskrity, Paul V.
1993   *Language, History, and Identity: Ethnolinguistic Studies of the Arizona Tewa.* Tucson: University of Arizona Press.

La Farge, Oliver
1966   Vidal Gutierrez. In *The Man with the Calabash Pipe,* 159–61. Boston: Houghton Mifflin.

Lange, Charles H.
1976   Obituary for W.W. Hill. *American Anthropologist* 78(1): 87–89.

La Potin, Armand S.
1987   *Native American Voluntary Organizations.* New York: Greenwood Press.

Laski, Vera
1958   *Seeking Life.* Memoirs of the American Folklore Society, vol. 50. Philadelphia.

LeBar, Frank M.
1968   Review of *Mountain Arbiters: The Changing Life of a Philippine Hill People,* by Edward P. Dozier. *Ethnohistory* 2(3): 277–79.

Longacre, William A., and James M. Skibo, eds.
1994   *Kalinga Ethnoarchaeology: Expanding Archaeological Method and Theory.* Washington, DC: Smithsonian Institution Press.

Lowie, Robert H.
n.d.   Review of *The Hopi-Tewa of Arizona,* by Edward P. Dozier (in German). *Sociologus,* n.s., year 6, vol. 2.

Maher, Robert F.
1968   Review of *The Kalinga of Northern Luzon, Philippines,* by Edward P. Dozier. *American Anthropologist* 70(3): 598–99.

Marriott, Alice
1948   *Maria: The Potter of San Ildefonso.* Norman: University of Oklahoma Press.

McNickle, D'Arcy
1971   *Indian Man: A Life of Oliver La Farge.* Bloomington: Indiana University Press.

Medicine, Beatrice
1973   Anthropologists and American Indian Studies Programs. In *Anthropology and the American Indian: A Symposium,* 75–84. San Francisco: Indian Historical Press.

Mihesuah, Devon A.
1998   *Natives and Academics: Researching and Writing about American Indians.* Lincoln: University of Nebraska Press.

Momaday, N. Scott
1968   *House Made of Dawn.* New York: Harper and Row.

Naranjo, Tessie
1992   Social Change and Pottery-Making at Santa Clara Pueblo. Ph.D. dissertation, University of New Mexico, Albuquerque.

Naranjo-Morse, Nora
1992   *Mud Woman: Poems from the Clay.* Sun Tracks, vol. 20. Tucson: University of Arizona Press.

Newsweek
1952   Dozier Dossier. *Newsweek* 39 (March 24): 67–68.

Norcini, Marilyn
1988   The Education of a Native American Anthropologist: Edward P. Dozier (1916–1971). Master's thesis, Department of Anthropology, University of Arizona, Tucson.
1995   Edward P. Dozier: A History of Native American Discourse in Anthropology. Ph.D. dissertation, Department of Anthropology, University of Arizona, Tucson.

Ortiz, Alfonso
1965   Dual Organization as an Operational Concept in the Pueblo Southwest. *Ethnology* 4(4): 389–96.
1966   Review of *Hano: A Tewa Indian Community in Arizona,* by Edward P. Dozier. *American Anthropologist* 68(5): 1295–96.
1969   *The Tewa World: Space, Time, Being, and Becoming in a Pueblo Society.* Chicago: University of Chicago Press.

Ortiz, Alfonso, ed.
1972   *New Perspectives on the Pueblos.* Albuquerque: University of New Mexico Press.

Parker, Dorothy
1992 *Singing an Indian Song: A Biography of D'Arcy McNickle.* Lincoln: University of Nebraska Press.

Parsons, Elsie Clews
1929 *The Social Organization of the Tewa of New Mexico.* Memoirs of the American Anthropological Association, no. 36. Menasha, WI: George Banta.

Prucha, Francis Paul, ed.
1975 *Documents of United States Indian Policy.* Lincoln: University of Nebraska Press.

Raushenbush, Esther
1972 John Hay Whitney Foundation: A Report of the First Twenty-five Years, vol. 1. New York: John Hay Whitney Foundation.

Reed, Eric K.
1943 The Origins of Hano Pueblo. *El Palacio* 50(4): 73–76.
1952 The Tewa Indians of the Hopi Country. *Plateau* 25(1): 11–18.

Rideout, Henry Milner
1912 *William Jones: Indian, Cowboy, American Scholar, and Anthropologist in the Field.* New York: Frederick A. Stokes.

Riley, Mary, ed.
2004 *Indigenous Intellectual Property Rights: Legal Obstacles and Innovative Solutions.* Walnut Creek, CA: Altamira Press.

Rogge, A. E.
1976 A Look at Academic Anthropology: Through a Graph Darkly. *American Anthropology* 78(4): 829–43.

Rosaldo, Renato
1980 *Ilongot Headhunting, 1883–1974: A Study in Society and History.* Stanford, CA: Stanford University Press.

Santa Clara Pueblo
1935 Constitution and Bylaws of the Pueblo of Santa Clara, New Mexico. Approved December 20, 1935.

Seaton, Elizabeth P.
2001 The Native Collector: Louis Shotridge and the Contests of Possession. *Ethnography* 2(1): 35–62.

Sergeant, Elizabeth Shepley
1935 The Indian Pueblos. In *Tewa Basin Study,* vol. 1. Albuquerque: U.S. Soil Conservation Service, Region 8, Division of Economic Surveys.

Shotridge, Louis
1929 The Kaguanton Shark Helmet. *Museum Journal* (Museum of the University of Pennsylvania) 20(2): 339–43.

Singer, Milton
1976 Robert Redfield's Development of a Social Anthropology of Civilizations. In *American Anthropology, the Early Years,* ed. John V. Murra, 187–260. St. Paul, MN: West Publishing.

Smith, Claire, and H. Martin Wobst, eds.
2005   *Indigenous Archaeologies: Decolonizing Theory and Practice.* New York: Routledge.

Smith, Watson
1956   Review of *The Hopi-Tewa of Arizona,* by Edward P. Dozier. *American Antiquity* 21(3): 324–25.

Spicer, Edward H.
1962   *Cycles of Conquest: The Impact of Spain, Mexico, and the United States on the Indians of the Southwest, 1533–1960.* Tucson: University of Arizona Press.

Spicer, Edward H., ed.
1961   *Perspectives in American Indian Culture Change.* Chicago: University of Chicago Press.

Spindler, George, and Louise Spindler
1966   Foreword. In *Hano: A Tewa Indian Community in Arizona,* by Edward P. Dozier, v–vi. New York: Holt, Rinehart, and Winston.

Stauss, Jay, Mary Jo Tippeconnic Fox, and Shelly Lowe
2002   American Indian Studies at the University of Arizona. In *Native American Studies in Higher Education: Models for Collaboration between Universities and Indigenous Nations,* eds. Duane Champagne and Jay Stauss, 83–96. Walnut Creek, CA: Altamira Press.

Stocking, George W. Jr.
1992   *The Ethnographer's Magic and Other Essays in the History of Anthropology.* Madison: University of Wisconsin Press.

Swentzell, Rina (Naranjo)
1992   Levels of Truth: Southwest Archaeologists and Anasazi-Pueblo People. *Contact* (Southwestern Region Interpreters newsletter), January–March.

Takaki, Michiko
1969   Review of *Mountain Arbiters: The Changing Life of a Philippine Hill People,* by Edward P. Dozier. *American Anthropologist* 71(3): 515–18.

Tedlock, Dennis
1972   Review of *The Pueblo Indians of North America,* by Edward P. Dozier. *American Anthropologist* 74 (1–2): 32–34.

Thornton, Russell, ed.
1998   *Studying Native America: Problems and Prospects.* Madison: University of Wisconsin Press.

U.S. Congress
1958   Senate Congressional Committee, 85th Congress, Hearings on S1390-6. Refer to Edward P. Dozier Papers, subgroup 4.

White, Hayden
1978   *Tropics of Discourse: Essays in Cultural Criticism.* Baltimore, MD: Johns Hopkins University Press.
Wilson, Waziyatawin Angela, and Michael Yellow Bird, eds.
2005   *For Indigenous Eyes Only: A Decolonization Handbook.* Santa Fe: School of American Research Press.
Yava, Albert
1978   *Big Falling Snow: A Tewa-Hopi Indian's Life and Times and the History and Traditions of His People.* Edited and annotated by Harold Courlander. New York: Crown.
Yearbook of Anthropology
1955   Ed. William L. Thomas Jr. New York: Wenner-Gren Foundation for Anthropological Research.

Index

acculturation, 66–67, 74, 80–83
American Indian Chicago Conference, 113–114
American Indian "civilization regulations," 24
American Indian faculty, 127–128, 132–134
American Indian higher education, 37
American Indian scholars (academics, government, museum), 8–11, 77, 135–136, 145. *See also* paradox
American Indian Studies (AIS), 37, 113–134, 140
"anthropological other," 95–96, 111
Arizona State University, 120
Arizona Tewa (Hopi-Tewa), 55–75
Association of American Indian Affairs (AAIA), 89–92, 121

Barton, Roy Franklin, 98–99, 109
Basso, Keith, 26–27, 132, 135
Boas, Franz, 6, 10
Boasian anthropologists, 6, 10–11, 49, 56–57
Bodine, John J., 5, 136
books: Pueblo perspectives on, 7–8
Bureau of Ethnic Research, 116–117
Bureau of Indian Affairs (BIA), 10, 33, 39

Butler, Claire Elizabeth (Betty). *See* Dozier, Claire Elizabeth Butler

Chamorro, 46
Chaudhur, Joyotpaul, 130
citizenship, 20, 30
civil rights movement, 114–115, 119
clans: Arizona Tewa, 70–72; Badger clan at Santa Clara Pueblo, 17, 65; clan relatives and kinship ties, 64–65, 73; Hopi, 71
Collier, John, 28, 32
compartmentalization, 83–85

Deloria, Vine, Jr., 61, 133, 136
Dozier, Claire Elizabeth Butler, 46, 49
Dozier, Leocadia Gutierrez, 15–23, 30; prenuptial agreement, 20–22, 163–166.
Dozier, Marianne Fink, 65–66, 72, 79
Dozier, Thomas Sublette, 15–23; and prenuptial agreement with Leocadia Dozier, 20–22, 163–166; pueblo day school teacher, 16, 31; relationship with Southwestern anthropologists, 65; Tewa language, 35–36

Eggan, Fred: on Philippine ethnography, 92–93, 96, 98, 101, 109; on Pueblo ethnography, 68
Ellis, Florence Hawley, 79, 85
ethnic studies programs, 114–115, 121, 129
Evers, Larry, 131

factionalism: Pueblo, 17, 70, 137
fellowships awarded to Dozier: by Guggenheim Foundation, 121; John Hay Whitney Opportunity Fellowship, 61, 138; by Social Science Research Council, 59, 93; by Stanford University Center for Advanced Studies, 89; by Wenner-Gren Foundation, 79, 88
Fink, Marianne. *See* Dozier, Marianne Fink
Fontana, Bernard, xix–xxi, 122
Ford Foundation, 123–133

GI Bill, 49, 77, 138
grants to American Indian Studies: by Ford Foundation, 123–133; by Rockefeller Foundation, 121
grants awarded to Dozier: by Ford Foundation Fund for Advancement of Education, 79, 138; by National Science Foundation, 93. *See also* fellowships awarded to Dozier

Hale, Kenneth, 132
Hano. *See* Tewa Village
Harrington, John P., 34, 50, 79
Haury, Emil, 27, 96, 113, 118
head-hunting: by the Ilingot, 110; by the Kalingas, 97–98, 107, 109
Herskovits, Melville, 80
Hill, W. W.: and Santa Clara Pueblo ethnography, 40–43, 66, 141–144; at the University of New Mexico, 40–44, 49, 79
Hoijer, Harry: at UCLA, 49–50, 53, 79; at the University of New Mexico, 44, 49–50
Hopi-Tewa. *See* Arizona Tewa
Hsu, Francis L. K., 81, 140

Indian Emergency Conservation Work program, 37
Indian Reorganization Act (IRA), 37, 39
indigenous anthropologists, 95–96, 143. *See also* American Indian anthropologists; American Indian scholars
"insider/outsider" relations, 4, 95, 111, 143

Jeançon, Jean Allard, 41–42
John Hay Whitney Opportunity Fellowship, 61, 138
Jones, William: as anthropologist, 77, 97; death of, 97, 101, 110

Kalingas, 92–93, 95–111; contrasted with Pueblos, 102–104; fieldwork among, 99–107; head-hunting by, 97–98, 107; peace pacts, 98, 107–108
kinship, 11; with the Hopi-Tewa, 64–65. *See also* clans
knowledge: Pueblo systems of, 4–5, 7–8
Krutz, Gordon, 117

La Farge, Oliver, 61–62, 79, 89
Lange, Charles H., 41, 43, 55–56, 142
Laski, Vera, 25
linguistics: study of ancestral Tewa, 34–36, 49–52; at UCLA, 56–57

McNickle, D'Arcy, 10, 61, 119, 136
moieties: at Santa Clara Pueblo, 16, 47–48
Momaday, N. Scott, 136, 139

National Science Foundation, 93
National Youth Administration, 41
Northwestern University, 80–81, 92

Ortiz, Alfonso, 5, 61, 136

paradox, 3–13, 135–137, 140
Parsons, Elsie Clews, 42, 66, 142
peace pact: Kalinga, 98, 107–108
"primitive": anthropological concepts of the, 85–88, 137
Pueblo Wild Flower Project, 33–35, 141

racial discrimination, 39–40, 113–114; segregation study, 79
reciprocity, 64, 65, 73
Rockefeller Foundation, 121

Saint Michael's College, 27–28
salvage ethnography, 5, 48
Santa Clara Pueblo: constitution of, 33, 38–39; ethnography of, 41–43, 48, 141–143; Elizabeth Shepley Sergeant and, 32–36, 52
secrecy, 4, 66–67, 142
Sekaquaptewa, Emory, 117, 122, 130
Sergeant, Elizabeth Shepley, 32–36, 52; and Pueblo Wild Flower Project, 33–35, 141
Shotridge, Louis, 9–10

Spicer, Edward H., 79–85; and compartmentalization, 83–85
Spier, Leslie, 79
Strauss, Joseph (Jay), 102

termination, Senate subcommittee hearing on, 89–92
Tewa: Arizona Tewa, 55–75; curse, 58, 68; language, 25, 33–36, 56; linguistics (Santa Clara), 49–52, 56; and Pueblo Wild Flower Project, 33–35, 141
Tewa Village (Hano), 12, 55–75, 79, 82, 83, 89
Thomas, Robert K., 133
Thompson, Raymond, 118, 121, 126–129

United Pueblo Agency, 33
United States Indian School (Albuquerque), 38
University of Arizona: Dozier at, 89, 94, 113–114; American Indian Studies at, 37, 113–134, 140
University of California, Los Angeles (UCLA), 52–53, 55–57
University of Minnesota, 120
University of New Mexico (UNM), 31, 38, 40, 49–53
University of Oregon, 78

Warren, David, 147–149
Weaver, Tom, 122
Wheeler Howard Act (48 Stat. 984), 37, 39
World War II, 46–48, 92

Yava, Albert, 62

About the Author

Marilyn Norcini is an interdisciplinary scholar who approaches research from the perspectives of anthropology, history, biography, material culture, and federal Indian law. She has graduate degrees from the University of Arizona in anthropology and American Indian Studies and the State University of New York at Oneonta, Cooperstown Graduate Program in history museum studies.

Norcini has worked in several museums in the Southwest and Northeast since 1975. She was the Director of the University Museum at New Mexico State University and Associate Director for Collections and Exhibitions at the University of Pennsylvania Museum of Archaeology and Anthropology, where she is currently a Senior Research Scientist in the American Section. She has also served as an ethnographer for applied projects with the National Park Service and the Los Alamos National Laboratory/DOE.

Norcini's research interests include American Indian history and culture, indigenous scholars, and the history of anthropology. She uses ethnographic and archival methods in her data collection. Currently, she is the Researcher Coordinator on a study of the history of Santa Clara Pueblo's 1935 constitution under the Indian Reorganization Act. The project is a collaborative research partnership between the Pueblo and the Penn Museum.